The IEA Health and Welfare Unit

Choice in Welfare No. 44

The Fragmenting Family: Does It Matter?

The IEA Health and Welfare Unit

Choice in Welfare No. 44

The Fragmenting Family: Does It Matter?

John Haskey
Kathleen Kiernan
Patricia Morgan

Miriam E. David (Editor)

IEA Health and Welfare Unit
London

First published June 1998

The IEA Health and Welfare Unit
2 Lord North St
London SW1P 3LB

Families: Their Historical Context, and Recent Trends
in the Factors Influencing Their Formation and Dissolution

ISBN 0-255 36436-9
ISSN 1362-9565

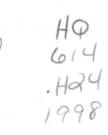

Typeset by the IEA Health and Welfare Unit
in Bookman 10 point
Printed in Great Britain by
St Edmundsbury Press Ltd
Bury St Edmunds, Suffolk

Contents

Page

The Authors   vi

Foreword
  David G. Green   viii

Editor's Introduction
  Miriam E. David   1

Families: Their Historical Context, and Recent Trends in the Factors Influencing Their Formation and Dissolution
  John Haskey   9

Figures
1 Live Births, 1900-95, England and Wales   34
2 Average Achieved Family Size of Women By Certain Ages,
   By Year of Birth of Women, 1924-75, England and Wales   35
3 Total Period Fertility Rate, 1938-95, England and Wales   36
4 Births Outside Marriage as a Percentage of All Live Births,
   1845-1995, England and Wales   37
5 Live Births Outside Marriage as a Percentage of All Live Births,
   1985-95, England and Wales   38
6 Marriages, 1845-1995, England and Wales   39
7 Percentage of Women Who Reported that They Had Pre-maritally
   Cohabited with Their Future Husband for (a) All First Marriages
   and (b) All Second Marriages, by Year of Marriage, Great Britain   40
8 Divorces and Divorce-related Series for Women, 1859-1995,
   England and Wales   41
9 Cumulative Percentages of Marriages which Ended in Divorce,
   by Marriage Cohort and Duration of Marriage, England and Wales   42
10 Percentages of All Families with Dependent Children Headed
   by Lone Mothers (by Their Marital Status) and by Lone Fathers,
   1971-95, Great Britain   43
11a Composition of Families by Type and Age of Head of Family,
   1991-94, Great Britain   44
11b Composition of One-Parent Families by Type and Age of Parent,
   1991-94, Great Britain   45

References   46

Commentaries

Family Change: Issues and Implications
  Kathleen Kiernan   51

An Endangered Species?
  Patricia Morgan   65

Notes   83

The Authors

John Haskey is a statistician/demographer who heads the Social Statistics Unit within the Demography and Health Division of the Office for National Statistics. He has responsibility for producing, analysing and publishing statistical information on a number of topics: marriage, divorce and cohabitation; families and households (including one-parent families and stepfamilies); adoptions; and ethnic minority and overseas-born populations. He has written on all these subjects, particularly on marriage, divorce and cohabitation, and on one-parent families.

Miriam E. David is Professor and Dean of Research at the London Institute. Previously she was Professor of Social Sciences and Director of the Social Sciences Research Centre at South Bank University, London, where she was also responsible for co-ordinating research across the university. She has recently served on the Higher Education Funding Council's (HEFCE) Research Assessment Exercise (RAE) sociology panel. Her recent publications include *Mother's Intuition? Choosing Secondary Schools*, with Anne West and Jane Ribbens, 1994 and *Educational Reforms and Gender Equality in Schools*, with Madeleine Arnot and Gaby Weiner, 1996. She is co-editor, with Dr Dulcie Groves, of *The Journal of Social Policy* and an executive editor of the *British Journal of the Sociology of Education*.

Kathleen Kiernan is Reader in Social Policy and Demography and a co-director of the ESRC Centre for the Analysis of Social Exclusion (CASE) at the London School of Economics and Political Science. She has written and researched widely on a range of issues relating to the family. Recent research has included an examination of the legacy of parental divorce, the rise of cohabitation and divorce, and changing patterns of parenthood. Books include *Lone Motherhood in the Twentieth Century*, with Hilary Land and Jane Lewis; *Cohabitation, Extra-marital Childbearing and Social Policy*, with Valerie Estaugh; and *Family Change and Social Policy*, with Malcolm Wicks.

Patricia Morgan, Senior Research Fellow in the family at the IEA Health and Welfare Unit, is a sociologist specialising in criminology and family policy. Her books include *Delinquent Fantasies*,

1978; *Facing Up to Family Income*, 1989; *Families in Dreamland*, 1992; *Farewell to the Family?*, 1995; *Are Families Affordable?*, 1996; *Who Needs Parents?*, 1996; and *Adoption and the Care of Children*, 1998. She has contributed chapters to *Full Circle*, *Family Portraits*, *The Loss of Virtue*, *Tried But Untested*, *Liberating Women from Modern Feminism* and *Just a Piece of Paper?*, as well as articles for periodicals and national newspapers. Patricia Morgan is a frequent contributor to television and radio programmes and is presently writing a full-length work on the relationship between capitalism and the family.

Foreword

This book has been designed primarily for school, college and university teaching. The leading essay is by John Haskey, the highly-respected statistician who heads the Social Statistics Unit within the Demography and Health Division of the Office for National Statistics (ONS).

The trends presented by John Haskey are then subjected to interpretation by three distinguished academic commentators. Miriam David, the Editor, provides a lively overview and Kathleen Kiernan concludes that the changing pattern of family life means that the focus of public policy should be on 'parenthood' rather than 'marriage contracts'.

Patricia Morgan, on the other hand, argues that the weakening of the husband-wife family as the primary method of raising children has been a change for the worse. We should not accept the continuation of this trend as if it were inevitable, but seek to reverse it.

All told, the authors provide an accessible introduction to the controversies about the future of the family and the raising of children that now regularly appear in our newspapers and broadcast media. And they offer valuable insights into the unanticipated effects of public policies on lifestyle choices which concern students of all the social sciences, from economics to sociology.

David G. Green

Editor's Introduction

Miriam E. David

IS the family changing, fragmenting, breaking up or down? And how do we know which, what or how? The family, how to define it, who are family members, whether it is changing, why and how, are all subject to public debate and scrutiny at present. This kind of debate has been raging for over two decades now, but it has become increasingly intense in the last few years as changes in rates and forms of marriage, divorce, parenthood and childbearing, household formation and dissolution etc. appear to be occurring. However, much of this debate has focused on moral censure or outrage over some aspects of the so-called 'problem of the family', such as cohabitation rather than marriage, and births out-of-wedlock rather than to married parents, possibly creating single-parent households. Evidence for these moral dilemmas, their causes and/or consequences, has not been uppermost in the public debate. Rather there has been concern to stem the tide and prevent what is seen as fragmentation or erosion of the family. Indeed an array of proposals to develop public policies for supporting certain traditional families and against emerging families which do not conform to traditional and often religious stereotypes has proliferated.

In particular, the new Labour government came to power in May 1997 with a policy agenda that placed the family at the heart of its proposals. For example, 'education, education, education' was the central plank of domestic policies as Tony Blair, the incoming Prime Minister, asserted. Indeed, the first policy document of the new Government was on education and its relationship with families. David Blunkett, the Secretary of State for Education and Employment, made the relationship crystal clear in his foreword to the white paper *Excellence in Schools*:

1

Excellence can only be achieved on the basis of **partnership**. We all need to be involved: schools, teachers and parents are at the heart of it. We also need the help of all of you. Families and the wider community.[1]

On the other hand, however, the proposals to reform the welfare state have centred on attempts to change some aspects of the family. A new category of recipients of social security has been named by the new Labour government and proposals developed for this so-called group of *'lone mothers'*: mothers with dependent children mainly in early childhood education, either at primary or nursery school. Although the notion of 'naming and shaming' has not specifically been used in this arena, but generally for education, it is an apposite attribution here too. In November 1997, as a prelude to debate on welfare reforms, a proposal to cut social security benefits to lone mothers was presented to Parliament by the Secretary of State for Social Security, Harriet Harman. Despite considerable protest by over 50 backbench Labour MPs, it was passed. A pilot project to get lone mothers to take up paid work rather than depend upon benefits was also developed as part and parcel of the initial welfare reforms in the summer of 1997. Indeed, one of the major targets of the programme of 'Welfare to Work' has been these so-called lone mothers, shaming them for their dependence upon social welfare and requiring them to obtain work instead of remaining as full-time mothers.

These policy proposals for both education and social security drew on an agenda that had been developed by the previous Conservative administrations. The Conservatives had also mixed *partnership* and *punishment* in equal measure in attempts to deal with what was seen as the burgeoning 'problem of the family'. They too had relied on families to choose schools to improve educational standards, on the one hand, naming their strategy one of *parental choice,* and penalized those families who did not have a male head of household and/or an adequate income from employment, on the other hand. However they did not name the problem in the way in which the Labour government has done but relied on the general concept of two-parent and lone-parent families, shaming all such families about their dependence on social welfare.

The twin strategies for families of partnership and punishment as a basis for public policies had developed with scant regard for the evidence about the causes of these family dilemmas, nor with a view to the consequences of such policies for family life. Most importantly, however, they took as given the fact that families were changing and that some 'problem' or 'problematic' families were becoming a charge on the public purse that was too high to bear. Hence the policy proposal to punish some such families whilst at the same time expect those very same families, *inter alia*, to share a partnership with government over raising educational standards. But just what is the case for arguing that there is now a so-called 'problem of the family' and that the family is in the process of fragmenting? How do we know what it is and how it has occurred and what should be done about it?

The aim of this book is to present first a clear and concise review of the evidence that has been accumulated to demonstrate changing rather than fragmenting family forms, and second to present two contrasting perspectives on that evidence, somewhat akin to the two approaches outlined above. On the one hand, a case will be made for revising family policies to take account of particular changes and developing a *partnership* approach, and on the other an argument will be presented on the deleterious consequences of certain changes in family life as fragmentation requiring a *punishment* perspective.

It is timely that the IEA has asked John Haskey to provide a review of the evidence from an official perspective, that of the Office for National Statistics. As usual he provides us with a measured account of families in historical context, with a commentary on the recent trends in the factors influencing their formation and dissolution. His picture is complex and carefully presented, together with a thoughtful comment on the methodology and characteristics of the sources of the evidence used. From this complicated set of trends it is not possible to assert simply that the family is fragmenting. Rather Haskey cautions us to look at the cross-cutting patterns that have emerged.

Haskey draws our attention to twelve key features of these emerging patterns over this century from, to pick out just five of his composite bullet points: 'women having fewer children, childbearing at older ages and increasing childlessness' to 'growth in living alone' to 'decline in adult mortality; lower prevalence of widowed lone parenthood and increased proportion of families spanning two, three or more generations' to 'decline in adoption and growth in lone motherhood amongst never-married women' to 'increase in the proportion of remarriages amongst all marriages and the consequent growth in married-couple step-families' (see p. 11). However, I think it is important from the point of view of the emerging policy debate to highlight just three salient features of this complex and complicated patterning of family forms. These are all to do with the changing features and characteristics of women's lives in families, which have in fact been targeted by policy analysts.

First is the shift in fertility patterns, such that, for the first time over the last two centuries for which we have the evidence, the fertility rate for women in their early thirties has overtaken that of women in their early twenties. Haskey states:

> This pattern reflects a change over recent years in the *timing* of childbearing, with a tendency to delay having children (p. 15).

In other words, more women are now delaying motherhood than in the past, which is thus altering the typical age of family formation and especially that of motherhood. Haskey offers us some reasons why this may be the case:

> the increased proportion of women undertaking higher education; more young women continuing to work and develop their careers before starting a family; and easier control over fertility by use of contraception (p. 15).

Haskey's reasons are a clear mix of public policy developments, such as the expansion of educational opportunities into higher education, family planning policy developments dependent upon technological innovations, and economic changes allowing women to enter and remain in the labour market. Whatever the causes, Haskey points to a new pattern in motherhood for this and probably subsequent generations.

Second, Haskey points us to the overarching context in which women are now bearing their children, that is *outside* rather than *inside* marriage. He says:

> There has been an exceptional rise during the last two decades in the proportion of all births which take place outside marriage...rising from nine per cent in 1976 to 34 per cent in 1995 (pp. 18-19).

He draws our attention to the fact that, although over a third of all births now take place outside marriage, a woman 'does not automatically become a lone mother'. He has a particular definition of lone motherhood here which is of mothers living alone, rather than being single, i.e. never married, or cohabiting.

He goes on to say: 'If she is living with the child's father—or another man—the couple form a cohabiting-couple family'. Again he points us to the complex family patterns that may come into existence in this context.

> It is likely that a birth registered solely by the mother indicates that she is a lone mother; similarly it is likely that the mother is a lone mother in jointly registered births where both parents have given *different* residential addresses. In contrast, jointly registered births where both parents live at the *same* address could well signify that the birth was to a cohabiting couple. These conclusions are very tentative and, of course, refer only to the circumstances at the time of the child's birth registration. The situation could well alter within a few months of the child's birth (p. 19).

He also points out that the almost two-thirds of births which occur *within marriage* are not all to a first-marriage mother but that some five per cent were to a remarried mother. This indicates another pattern that has been occurring, namely dramatic trends in marriage, divorce and remarriage alongside of cohabitation in place of legal marriage.

Thus, the third key feature of the patterns which I wish to highlight from Haskey's overall picture is that of the contrasting trends in the legal and non-legal institutions for parenthood and particularly motherhood. In other words, putting together the patterns of the age of motherhood with those of household formation or living arrangements, it is found that:

> the proportions of men and women who are married have consistently declined, whilst the proportions cohabiting have progressively increased...In addition, there has been another trend—a growing proportion of men and women who have *not* been living in a partnership (p. 23).

Haskey then goes on to complicate the picture with evidence about the trends in marriage, divorce and remarriage. He thus finds:

> two contrasting trends; married-couple families accounted for...of all families...71 per cent in 1994...whereas cohabiting-couple families formed...11 per cent in 1994...it is clear that the proportions of those with dependent children changed more quickly than those with non-dependent children only...A similar type of situation also occurred for lone-parent families (p. 28).

He again provides us with explanations for these trends based upon a mix of generational and policy effects. The overall picture however is that more children are born outside of the legal institution of marriage and grow up in families where there are changing patterns of parenthood, with cohabitation and remarriage as important as marriage. The significance is that dependent children may acquire more rather than fewer significant other adults as parents and/or step-parents throughout their childhood, whether or not those adults are legally related to them. In other words, lone motherhood is more of a snapshot than a moving picture throughout a child's period of dependency. Haskey concludes that it is not possible simply to read off from these diverse patterns what the future of family life is or will be. He invites us to consider the rich complexity.

Kathleen Kiernan's essay picks up some of these rich patterns and develops an argument about the ways in which public policies might be developed to take account of growing diversity and individualism, especially economic individualism. She also extends the picture to include the changing economic context for affecting family life, especially focusing on women's changing economic behaviour. Drawing on comparative evidence, in particular that from Sweden, she pinpoints as possible public policy measures the ways in which legal institutions might consider marriage and cohabitation. She also raises, more saliently, how to deal with the question of the changing patterns of parenthood, and especially motherhood, for both women and their children. She suggests a renegotiation of the relationship between work and families for considering children's well-being. She stresses, however, the importance for public policy developments of parenthood, and especially motherhood, rather than the issues of the legality or otherwise of such parental living arrangements. In other words, she is at pains to argue for family-friendly public policies which support mothers' labour-force participation and partnerships with, amongst others, the state. She is thus arguing against those who would propose policies to reverse the tide of history with respect to the sole significance of marriage and legal motherhood.

Patricia Morgan wants to reinvigorate the moral arguments with a revisiting of the nature-versus-nurture debates. She picks out some points from Haskey's evidence with a surprising postmodernist skill. Indeed, referring to 'post-modern optimism', she turns herself into what might be considered a 'born again' postmodernist and attends only to the detail with which she is interested rather than to the consistent and coherent flow of Haskey's 'modernist' and rationalist argument. At another level, or in another language, it is possible to consider her a very worried woman, worried that *homo sapiens*, as we have 'traditionally' known him, might die out. Indeed her piece is called 'An Endangered Species?' She points to a declining birth rate and a parallel declining marriage rate, such that of the decreasing numbers of children born now increasing numbers are to be found in out-of-wedlock rather than traditional married-couple households/families.

Thus she raises her key worry which is what is happening to the role of men, particularly fathers. She wants to ensure the reassertion of a patriarchal order and she argues for a return to the world we have lost. She does not acknowledge that the development of a small number of what we might call *father-free zones* are ones which women themselves may have chosen in order to free themselves from sexual abuse and harassment. She suggests a number of strategies to reverse these particular patterns, in particular by celebrating the institution of marriage. She also implies that women who choose lone parenthood are recalcitrant and that they should not be rewarded through the benefits system if they choose not to marry. Her grounds are that such patterns are a major strain on public resources, but she has not conducted what might be considered a comprehensive cost-benefit analysis of these complex family patterns. Nor has she, or could she, estimate how much it would cost for the public purse to pursue such punitive family policies rather than support partnership policies.

What this edited collection offers our readers is a mixture of evidence and policy proposals for how to deal with the family. We invite you to consider here whether indeed the family is changing or fragmenting, and whether it matters; and, if it does matter, how we can deal with it mattering by policies to support or punish parents to help create the future generations. We hope that these three chapters will stimulate debate, challenge accepted orthodoxies and provoke new ideas for a family-friendly future.

Families: Their Historical Context, and Recent Trends in the Factors Influencing Their Formation and Dissolution

John Haskey

Summary

This chapter gives some statistical information on how the family has changed in recent decades and on its contemporary characteristics. The subjects of fertility, marriage, cohabitation and divorce are explored, and their effects upon the changing profile of families are discussed. Some related phenomena are also mentioned, such as the growth in living alone, and the decline in several families sharing the same household.

Introduction

THE family has been the subject of increasing scrutiny in recent years, since everyone is aware that families are under stress with the incidence of marital breakdown and lone parent-hood having grown considerably in the last generation. As a result, the diversity of family forms has increased in recent decades, with 'traditional' families in relative numerical decline. There have been many changes this century which have had a direct bearing upon the family—in particular, a number of trends which can be traced back to the 1960s, when the seeds of many subsequent developments seem to have been sown.

The family is arguably the most important institution we have; for children it offers the secure environment in which to develop physically and emotionally, whilst, for parents, families provide the forum for love, care, mutual support, fulfilment and well-being as adults, as well as a well-tested framework in which to bring up children. From society's viewpoint, it is perhaps this latter role which is crucial; families provide the natural habitat in which children learn the necessary social skills to live with

9

others—brothers, sisters, parents and childhood friends, and subsequently, beyond the childhood home, as well-adjusted adults, integrated into society.

Data sources

This chapter presents some statistical information on social trends which have had a direct effect upon people, families and households; for example, the trends in fertility, marriage, divorce, and cohabitation. Whilst an interpretative description based on statistical data can provide an *overall* picture of social developments, it cannot, unaided, give an impression of the immense variety of family circumstances and situations which exist. The main reason is the lack of detail, since only certain items of information are collected, and for subjects such as fertility, marriage and divorce, these items, derived from registration systems, are collected primarily for the legal purpose of recording the events and identifying the people involved, rather than for documenting contemporary social trends.

Other data sources, such as the census and social surveys, do, however, collect summary information specifically for the purpose of obtaining a 'social snapshot' of the number and characteristics of people, families and households. These latter data sources provide key details on people and families; the census captures data on all of them, and surveys on representative samples of them.

For particular purposes where relevant data do not exist, or where there is insufficient detail, information from in-depth case studies can sometimes very usefully complement the available data, although such cases are usually special in some way—that is, not strictly representative of all individuals or all families. There will be little subsequent mention of data sources in this chapter although some references are given at the end.

A parallel can be drawn to illustrate the process of using the available data sources to identify and describe social change. The task of the historian is to find and evaluate surviving material and use the appropriate techniques to paint as complete a picture of the past as possible. In just the same way, the demographer,* or social statistician, has to obtain and analyse the

---

* Someone who studies the subject of population

available statistical evidence in order to detect, understand and report the most significant events and trends. This process is perhaps best exemplified by the historical research on families and households which has been carried out using a variety of alternative data sources and reconstruction techniques. The fruits of all this scholarship have enabled the contemporary pattern of family living—and the changes witnessed in recent decades—to be viewed from a broader historical perspective.

Main Changes Affecting Families This Century

It is useful, at the outset, to list the main demographic changes which have occurred this century which have had an impact upon families and households:

- Women having fewer children, childbearing at older ages and increasing childlessness
- Advent of modern contraception and increased use of abortion
- Smaller household and family sizes
- Decline in extended families and multi-family households; overall fewer kin
- Growth in living alone
- Fall in infant mortality resulting in virtually all children surviving to adulthood
- Decline in adult mortality; lower prevalence of widowed lone parenthood and increased proportions of families spanning two, three or more generations
- Increased numbers of elderly, who either live alone, in institutions or with their children or relatives
- Decline in adoption and growth in lone motherhood amongst never-married women
- Increase in births outside marriage and consequent growth in cohabiting-couple families and lone parenthood
- Rise in the prevalence of cohabitation, decline in first marriage and growth in divorce
- Increase in the proportion of remarriages amongst all marriages and the consequent growth in married-couple stepfamilies
- Growth in cohabitation of lone parents with new partners; the creation of cohabiting-couple stepfamilies

Of course, all of these trends—some of which have been rapid and significant, others comparatively slow and of lesser importance—have had a collective and cumulative effect, and as such are interrelated.

In addition, the changes themselves can often bring about a new set of social attitudes, initially held by a few, and then by a growing number. A new social norm begins to be established which eventually leads to the norm gaining widespread acceptance. Further, since a new set of social attitudes is generally reflected in a new pattern of demographic behaviour, the process can be reinforcing. Examples might include attitudes towards childbearing outside marriage, and pre-marital cohabitation.

The following sections will consider the topics of fertility, mortality, marriage, divorce and cohabitation—factors which are the major determinants of the size and characteristics of families. Unless otherwise stated, the commentary, data and graphs will refer to England and Wales as a whole.

Fertility

Fertility is the most important determinant of both the number of people aged under 50 in the population and the profile of their ages—both of which influence the numbers of families and children within them. (Mortality plays some part, but nowadays it only really begins to come into play after about age 50.) The annual number of births has varied considerably over the years, with major peaks after the two world wars and in 1964, whilst there were deep troughs in 1933, 1941 and 1977 (see Figure 1, p. 34).

To an appreciable extent, peaks and troughs in births tend to be repeated one generation later as the original number of babies—either large or small in number—themselves become parents for the first time. However, the second peak or trough tends to be less distinct in shape than the first. The reason is because the women born in a particular peak or trough year have their first child at a variety of different ages, not all at the same age, and so in a variety of years, not all in the same year. Also, the same group of women have differing numbers of children, and at different intervals of time between children. For example, women born in 1947 began having children in the early 1960s, and only completely finished their childbearing during the early 1990s.

The number of births in a given year depends partly upon how many women there are of childbearing ages—usually taken as ages 15 to 44—and partly upon their fertility; that is, the proportion of them who give birth in a given year. Women in their late twenties have the highest fertility rates, with progressively older women having successively lower fertility rates. (The fertility rate for women of a given age-group is the annual number of births they have, per thousand of their number.) The number of births also depends, at least in more recent times, on women's decisions concerning the timing of births, the total number of children they wish to have, and their marital status—whether or not they are married, and, if so, whether they are in their first or subsequent marriage. These factors play a large part, as also do economic and social influences such as men's and women's incomes, patterns of employment, and aspirations concerning family life and lifestyle.

Average Family Size

Information on births can be analysed in terms of women's family sizes—in particular, the average number of children born per woman by age 45. Tracing this average family size for women born in successive years gives a summary picture of the changing size of families.

There have been some large changes in the last 150 years or so—the period covered by the national civil registration system for births, marriages and deaths. For example, women born in England and Wales in 1841 had, on average, almost three children each before they were 45. However, this average number of children, expressing as it does the number of births as a multiple of the original number of women born in 1841, was achieved despite the fact that almost one third of these women died before reaching age 15, and a further one in six died between the ages of 15 and 45. If none of these women had died, and instead they had had the same fertility as those who had lived, the average number of children per woman would have been five, rather than three. This is a substantial difference which shows the large effect of mortality upon women's fertility just over a century ago. In turn, of course, a proportion of these women's children died—over one quarter of children born in 1870 died before they were ten. Consequently, the population kept rising only because the number of births outpaced the number of deaths—and both were relatively high by today's standards. However, women's mortality up to age 45 lessened in impact in successive decades of the latter half of the last century, as death rates fell.

The average number of children born per woman fell steadily for women born in the years following 1841, from 2.9 to a low point of around 1.4 children per woman for women born around 1910. (This latter group of women reached the start of their childbearing years at the start of the Depression and were 35 by the time the Second World War had ended.) The average family size subsequently rose for women born in successive years up to the mid-1930s when a peak of 2.3 children per woman was reached. Since then, family sizes have declined, and although women born between 1950 and the mid-1960s have yet to complete their childbearing, their fertility rates to date suggest that the decline will continue at least for women born in years up to the mid-1960s.

Trends in Fertility Rates and Ages of Mothers at Childbirth

Considering the total number of births a woman has had by the end of her childbearing years gives an overall picture of completed family sizes, but gives no information about the ages at which the women had their children. It is estimated that the most striking falls in fertility rates last century—after about 1870 when fertility rates were at their peak—were amongst women aged 35 or over. Declining proportions of women were having four or more children, and it is reasonable to conclude that family limitation was becoming more and more widespread. However, fertility rates fell consistently in *every* age-group from 1871 to 1931 when the fertility rates for women under 30 were at a particularly low level, probably the result of the prevailing severe economic situation and widespread unemployment.

Not surprisingly, fertility rates rose sharply immediately after the Second World War in every age-group, then fell back in the early 1950s, but subsequently climbed to post-war peak values in 1964. After 1964 fertility rates declined abruptly to reach, in 1977, the lowest recorded this century. The sharpest falls occurred for women in their twenties and early thirties. Since about 1980, the overall level of fertility has been fairly stable, although fertility rates for younger women have continued to fall, whilst those for women aged over 30 have risen. Indeed, recently, for the first time, the fertility rate for women in their early thirties has overtaken that of women in their early twenties. This pattern reflects a change over recent years in the *timing* of childbearing, with a tendency to delay having children.

Evidence for this delay is found in the fact that the average age of women giving birth in the years from 1974 to 1994 has consistently risen, such that mothers in 1994 were, on average, two years older than their counterparts twenty years earlier. In addition, over the decade 1984 to 1994, the average age of mothers having their *first* birth also rose by two years, and the average ages of the different groups of mothers having their second, third and fourth births all increased, too. The reasons for this delay in childbearing are thought to include: the increased proportion of women undertaking higher education; more young women continuing to work and develop their careers before starting a family; and easier control over fertility by use of contraception.

Childlessness

An increasing proportion of women born in successive years after the Second World War have never had children. For example, among women born in 1946, 11 per cent were childless at the age of 35, but the corresponding proportions for women born in 1949, 1951, 1954 and 1959 were about 15, 18, 20, and 23 per cent, respectively. Of course, it is impossible to deduce how much of this childlessness has been voluntary, and how much has been due to an inability to have children. However, the fact that there was a range of new medical treatments available for infertility during the 1980s suggests that a large part was due to choice.

A recent study indicated that childlessness may be related to late age at marriage and high levels of marital breakdown, and, more indirectly, to such factors as women being highly qualified, or in a higher social class. Certainly results from surveys suggest that higher proportions of highly qualified women expect to be childless than other women. Survey results also show that, in general, women with more educational qualifications started childbearing at a later age and had smaller families than women with fewer educational qualifications.

Family-building—Average Family Size at Different Ages of Women

So far, discussion has centred on the average completed family sizes of previous generations of women, and the changes which have occurred during the last century in the fertility rates of women at different ages. As well as affecting the eventual size of women's families, the changes in women's fertility rates have also resulted in changes in the *pace* and *timing* with which women have completed their families. A straightforward way of summarising the information on this subject is to consider the average family sizes which were achieved *by different ages* of women throughout their childbearing years. Table 1 gives such average family sizes separately for groups of women born in successive years. The same data are also depicted in Figure 2, p.35.

Table 1
Average family size achieved by women by certain ages, by year of birth of women, 1929-74, England and Wales

| Year of birth of women | Average number of children per woman by age: | | | | | |
	20	25	30	35	40	45
1924	0.14	0.85	1.37	1.87	2.07	2.11
1929	0.19	0.90	1.61	2.05	2.23	2.26
1934	0.20	1.04	1.88	2.28	2.41	2.42
1939	0.26	1.22	1.98	2.27	2.35	2.36
1944	0.34	1.24	1.88	2.11	2.20	2.21
1949	0.35	1.09	1.67	1.96	2.06	2.08
1954	0.33	0.93	1.54	1.88	2.00	
1959	0.24	0.82	1.43	1.81		
1964	0.20	0.71	1.30			
1969	0.22	0.69				
1974	0.22					

It may be seen that there has been a marked decline in the average family size achieved by women at the younger ages. For example, by age 25, women born in 1944 had had, on average, 1.24 children, but women born twenty years later, in 1964, had only had 0.71 children. By age 30, the same two groups of women had had 1.88 and 1.30 children, respectively.

Similarly, there has been a decline in the average family sizes achieved by women by the middle of their childbearing years; the

average number of children per woman, by age 30, fell contin-
uously for women born in successive years after 1939. For
example, by age 30 the average family size for women born in
1944 was 1.88, but was 1.54 amongst women born in 1954. For
the same two groups of women, their average family sizes were
2.20 and 2.00 children, respectively, by the time the women were
40.

However, although average family sizes declined amongst
successive groups of women, there was a small amount of
'catching-up' when the women were in their thirties. In the
example just given, it can be seen that the women born in 1944
had, on average, 0.32 children during their thirties (0.32=2.20-
1.88), whilst the women born ten years later in 1954 had, on
average, 0.46 children (0.46=2.00-1.54) during their thirties, a
larger increase. This phenomenon suggests that later groups of
women have deferred their childbearing to older ages, although,
as the final column of Table 1 and Figure 2 (p. 35) show, the final
family sizes, by age 45, have continued to fall.

Total Fertility

The above analysis shows that we can only be sure of the
eventual family size of women who have already reached aged 45.
Hence, as can be seen from Table 1, the latest group of women
whose completed family sizes are definitely known are for those
who were born in 1949—they were 45 in 1994. However, we are
often more interested in the likely eventual family sizes of
younger women: those born in the 1950s, 1960s and 1970s. We
know how many children on average they have had in their early
years of childbearing, but not in their later years—because that
time is in the future. Of course, we can make assumptions about
their future fertility rates as part of a projections exercise, and
compute their implied completed family sizes, but the accuracy
of such projections is only as reliable as the assumptions upon
which they are based.

Another way of summarising the available information on
fertility involves considering all the fertility rates in a given
year—that is, the fertility rates for women aged between 15 and
19, 20 and 24, and so on, up to 40 to 44. An imaginary group of
women is then assumed to have births at exactly the same rate
as each of these fertility rates in turn. That is, between the ages
of 15 and 19, they have between them the number of births

predicted by the fertility rates for 15- to 19-year-olds for the year in question; then between the ages of 20 and 24 they have the number of births predicted by the fertility rate of 20- to 24-year-olds for the year in question, and so on, up to age 40 to 44. The total number of births this hypothetical group of women would have had by the time they reach age 45 can then be found, from which the average number of children per woman can be calculated. This average completed family size is based on the assumption that the women successively experience all the fertility rates observed in a given year. It is called the total period fertility rate because it essentially adds together the fertility rates of the given year, or period, so giving a summary measure of the observed fertility in that year. It is a useful index of what a given set of fertility rates would imply in the long run, rather than giving estimates or predictions for any *actual* group of women.

The total period fertility rate (TPFR) is plotted in Figure 3 (p. 36) for each year since 1938. Apart from the sharp peak in 1947 following the Second World War demobilisation, the TPFR remained close to a value of 2.1 until the mid-1950s. This particular value is special, and is called the replacement level. It is the level at which, in the long term, the number of births and deaths would balance if mortality rates were constant and migration—the balance of immigration and emigration—had no effect upon the population.

After the mid-1950s, the TPFR increased rapidly for ten years until a peak of 2.9 was reached in 1964. From 1964, the TPFR fell, just as abruptly as the earlier rise, to a trough value of 1.7 in 1977—the lowest level yet recorded for England and Wales. There was a slight rise in the TPFR to 1.9 between 1977 and 1980, but since then the level has remained fairly stable at around 1.8. However, it has fallen in each of the last four years to reach 1.7 in 1995.

For the last 20 years fertility has been below replacement level, although the size of the population is still growing slowly because the number of births and the net balance of immigration over emigration still exceed the number of deaths.

Births Outside Marriage

There has been an exceptional rise during the last two decades in the proportion of all births which take place outside marriage as Figure 4 (p. 37) shows. During the first 60 years of this century—apart from the two periods immediately after the two world wars—fewer than five per cent of births occurred outside marriage, but during the 1960s the proportion rose steadily, fluctuated around nine per cent in the late 1960s and early 1970s, and then maintained, over almost two decades, an extremely fast and consistent rate of increase, rising from nine per cent in 1976 to 34 per cent in 1995. Although a somewhat similar pattern has been observed in many European countries, the growth has been faster in England and Wales than in most other countries.

Of course, when a woman has a birth outside marriage, she does not automatically become a lone mother. If she is living with the child's father—or another man—the couple form a cohabiting-couple family. Another possibility, comparatively rare these days, but much more frequent thirty years or more ago, was for the mother to give her child up for adoption. Nowadays, however, most women giving birth outside marriage either become lone mothers or mothers within cohabiting-couple families with children. Of course, if the mothers have had children previously, they may already be in these types of families.

There is a little information from birth entries on the family circumstances of the mother and her child: some births are registered solely by the mother—that is, no details are recorded on the father—and others are registered jointly by both parents. In a sole registration of a birth, the mother's usual residential address is recorded, and, in a joint birth registration, the addresses of both the mother and father are recorded. It is likely that a birth registered solely by the mother indicates that she is a lone mother; similarly, it is likely that the mother is a lone mother in jointly registered births where the parents have given *different* residential addresses. In contrast, jointly registered births where both parents live at the *same* address could well signify that the birth was to a cohabiting couple. These conclusions are very tentative and, of course, refer only to the circumstances at the time of the child's birth registration. The situation could well alter within a few months of the child's birth.

Figure 5 (p. 38) shows the proportion of all births which took place outside marriage, distinguishing solely registered births from jointly registered births, and, amongst the latter, distinguishing identical parental address births from different parental address births. It may be seen that the bulk of the increase in the overall proportion of births outside marriage has been due to jointly registered births—and, in particular, in more recent years, to those in which the parents were living at the same address. (This finding is consistent with survey results which show a gradual increase in the proportion of cohabiting-couple families with dependent children amongst all families containing dependent children.) In contrast, the proportion of sole-registration births outside marriage has increased slightly and comparatively slowly. In 1985 under two-thirds (65 per cent) of births outside marriage were jointly registered by both parents, compared with over three-quarters (78 per cent) in 1995. Similarly, jointly registered *same-address* births accounted for under one-half (47 per cent) of all births outside marriage in 1985, but well over one-half (58 per cent) in 1995.

Births to Mothers in Their First, Second and Subsequent Marriages

Although the proportion of all births which have taken place outside marriage has grown dramatically in recent years, the majority—two thirds—still occur within marriage. However, because the incidence of divorce has also risen steeply over the last three decades, an increasing proportion of married women have been in their second—or subsequent—marriage. As a result, the proportion of all births which have been to remarried women has increased, from about two per cent in 1964 to five per cent in 1995. (Expressed as a proportion of all births *within marriage*, however, the increase is larger: from two per cent in 1964 to eight per cent in 1995.)

Hence, in 1995, overall, 61 per cent of births were to a mother within her first marriage; five per cent were to a remarried mother; and 34 per cent were to an unmarried mother. Since, together with fertility, marriage, divorce, remarriage and cohabitation are key factors in the formation and dissolution of families, these latter topics will now be considered.

Trends in Marriage, Divorce and Cohabitation

The annual number of marriages in England and Wales grew fairly steadily in the early decades of this century, punctuated only by the increase in marriages during and immediately after the two world wars—see Figure 6 (p. 39). However, the annual number fell sharply after a peak of over 400 thousand marriages in 1972. Apart from the special wartime situation in 1943, the annual number of marriages had not, until 1993, slipped below 300 thousand since the mid-1920s, when the Great Depression caused not only the economy to slow down, but the marriage rates to be depressed, too. The peaks and troughs around the time of the Depression and the two world wars are understandable given the prevailing circumstances; more generally, peaks can reflect marriages being brought forward in time, or a catching up, whilst troughs can reflect a postponement of marriage.

Figure 6 also shows that, since the early 1970s, the fall in the number of first marriages for both partners has been more headlong than for the total number of marriages, the number halving from a slightly earlier peak of 340 thousand in 1970 to 174 thousand in 1994. The number of such first marriages in 1994 was the lowest recorded this century; in fact the lowest since 1889, despite a much larger present-day population.

Of course, in any year, the difference between the total number of marriages and the number of first marriages for both partners gives the number of marriages in which one or both partners were remarrying. This difference is represented by the gap between the top two lines in Figure 6; for clarity it has also been plotted separately as the bottom line in Figure 6. It may be seen that, throughout the present century, the number of remarriages has generally increased. Early this century most remarriages involved a widow or a widower, whilst more recently the majority of remarriages took place with at least one partner who was divorced. This was particularly the case from the late 1960s and early 1970s when divorce rates rose rapidly.

Rates of Marriage

Considering the number of first marriages, or remarriages, is only the first step towards appreciating the underlying trends. Not only has the population grown in size—by which one would expect an *increasing* number of marriages—but its composition by age and marital status has changed. Considering *rates* of marriage by age and sex, separately for first marriages and remarriages—for example, the number of bachelors aged 20 to 24 marrying in a given year per thousand 20- to 24-year-old bachelors in the population that year, or the number of divorced women aged 35 to 39 remarrying per thousand such divorced women—identifies where the major changes have occurred.

Most of the marriage rates for bachelors and spinsters—for the different age-groups—were at high levels during the mid-1950s to late 1960s, which tended to make the subsequent declines appear particularly large. Since about 1970 the steepest falls in marriage rates for bachelors have been amongst those in their early and late twenties, and also in their teens, whereas the decline for those in their thirties has been relatively modest. The situation has been very similar for spinsters. More importantly, the marriage rates for both bachelors and spinsters, in almost every age-group, were lower in 1994 than they had been since before the Second World War. The only exceptions occurred for spinsters in their early and late thirties; their marriage rates in the early 1930s were slightly below those in 1994.

A similar story applies to rates of remarriage. There is a common pattern in which the younger the age-group, the steeper the fall in the remarriage rate since the early 1970s.

One important feature which applies equally to first marriages and remarriages, to men and to women, is that marriage rates have fallen considerably at the youngest ages—those under 30—without any sign of compensating increases in the older age-groups. If there *had* been such evidence, it would suggest that marriages have been increasingly postponed, rather than foregone, by an increasing minority of young men and women.

Age at First Marriage

There also is evidence that, amongst first marriages which have taken place, the bachelors and spinsters are older than their predecessors. For example, by the late 1960s bachelors were typically aged 23 at marriage, and spinsters 21, although these were the youngest ages at marriage since the Second World War. From about 1970, the ages of bachelors and spinsters at marriage rose consistently and at a quickening pace until they were over 27 and 25, respectively, for marriages in 1994—the oldest they had been for over 60 years.

Living Together

One contributory reason for the trend towards later first marriage has undoubtedly been the growth since the mid-1960s in the proportion of couples who have cohabited with their future marriage partner before marriage. Figure 7 (p. 40) illustrates the fact that the proportion of spinsters who lived with their future husband was very small—around five per cent—for those who married in the mid-1960s, but increased steadily to about 70 per cent of those who married in the early 1990s. The corresponding proportions were even higher for women who were marrying for the second time, increasing from around 30 per cent in the late 1960s to about 90 per cent for second marriages in the early 1990s.

The growing tendency to live together before first marriage has also been accompanied by a trend towards living together before first marriage for longer periods—and it is reasonable to conclude that these two factors have both contributed towards later age at first marriage.

In addition to the growing proportion of couples who lived together before marriage, there has also been a steadily rising proportion of men and women who have been cohabiting —whether or not that cohabitation has subsequently led to marriage, or will do so in the future. For example, about one in nine women aged from 18 to 49 who were not currently married were cohabiting in 1979; by 1993 this proportion had exactly doubled. Amongst the unmarried of the different marital statuses, the largest increases in the proportions cohabiting have been amongst bachelors and spinsters; for example, the proportion of spinsters aged from 18 to 49 who were cohabiting more than trebled from about one in 13 to one in four between 1979 and 1994. Despite this large increase, however, the corresponding proportion of divorced women who were cohabiting was slightly higher than for spinsters in 1994. However, amongst unmarried men and women, it has been divorced men who have cohabited in relatively greatest numbers—just under one half of those aged under 50 in recent years.

Perhaps not surprisingly, in the light of the results given above, the proportions of men and women who are married have consistently declined, whilst the proportions cohabiting have progressively increased. For example, in 1979 74 per cent of women aged from 18 to 49 were married and three per cent were cohabiting; in 1993 the proportions were 59 and nine per cent respectively. Furthermore, these trends have been more pronounced for those in their twenties. In addition, there has been another trend—a growing proportion of men and women who have *not* been living in a partnership, that is, *not* as a partner within either a married or cohabiting couple. Again this trend has been more pronounced amongst those in their twenties. In the example given immediately above, in 1979 23 per cent of women were neither married nor cohabiting; by 1993 this proportion had risen to 32 per cent. People in this category include those living with their parents, sharing a house or a flat with others, or living alone, or as a lone parent in a one-parent family. One of the ways in which men and women start to live on their own or with others is the result of divorce; divorce is also a major cause of lone parenthood which has risen steadily in recent decades. The subject of divorce will now be considered since it is the most important factor in the dissolution of families.

Divorce

The incidence of divorce has increased dramatically since an Act of Parliament in 1857 enabled divorce to be petitioned and granted in a civil court. (Before 1858, when the Act came into force, divorce could only be obtained by a private Act of Parliament, and so was available only to a wealthy few.)

In fact, since then, the increase in divorce has been immense; the present-day number of about 160 thousand couples divorcing each year in England and Wales is about one thousand times the annual number around 1870. As a result, a conventional graph depicting the numbers does not show very clearly where past increases occurred—because the scale has to be so large to accommodate the numbers for more recent years. This may be remedied using a logarithmic scale, and the number of divorces—and of some other related series—are shown this way in Figure 8 (p. 41). It can be seen that each interval along the y-axis in Figure 8 increases by a *factor* of 10, rather than by an *addition* of 10. Hence the increase from about 160 divorces per year to 160,000 per year is a 1,000-fold increase taking up three units on the y-axis: $1,000 = 10\text{x}10\text{x}10 = 10^3$. Over the period since civil divorce was first made possible, the annual numbers of divorces have, in general, tended to increase exponentially. Conveniently, an exponential increase shows up as a straight line when the data are plotted logarithmically, as in Figure 8. Figure 8 shows data for women only; those for men are either identical or very similar.

Although the married population of England and Wales has grown—approximately exponentially in the century up to 1951—its *rate* of increase, as measured by the gradient in Figure

8, is very much less than that for the annual number of divorces. In fact, the width of the gap between the two lines is related to the divorce rate; the closer the two lines, the higher the divorce rate. It may be seen that the gap has narrowed fairly consistently over the whole period from 1858, which is equivalent to the divorce rate rising exponentially. (Currently, the divorce rate is such that out of every 1,000 married couples, 14 married couples divorce each year.)

However, on closer inspection, the growth in the number of divorces can really be divided into four main periods, punctuated by the two world wars, and 1971 when there was a small, but decided, peak in divorces. The wars have had a greater effect upon the numbers of divorces than various legislative changes, although the repercussions of the latter have undoubtedly been longer lasting.

Also shown in Figure 8 are annual numbers of remarriages of divorced women. The path follows fairly closely that of divorces, although it might be noted that, contrary to what one might expect, there are few signs of a lag behind the number of divorces. The fact that historically there has always been a greater number of men and women divorcing than of those remarrying indicates that there has been a cumulation of divorced men and women in the population as the growth in the census-enumerated divorced population also indicates. The divorced population has risen relatively quickly since about 1971, and the gap between the numbers divorcing and remarrying after divorce has widened, indicating that an increasing proportion of the divorced are not remarrying; the divorced are increasingly living alone, or as divorced lone parents in one-parent families, or are cohabiting.

Finally, the numbers of those *re*-divorcing—that is, their previous marriage also ended in divorce—are also shown in Figure 8. The numbers rose exponentially in the period up to 1970 and at a faster rate after 1972. That their growth has been faster than the overall number divorcing is consistent with the finding that, age for age, the marriages of those previously divorced are more likely to end in divorce than those who marry for the first time.

Besides considering the overall divorce rate—the number of couples divorcing per thousand married couples in a given year—it is also possible to examine the divorce rates for married men and women in the different age-groups. For example, the divorce rate for married men aged 30 to 34 in 1994 is the number of such men who divorced that year per thousand married men who were aged 30 to 34 in 1994. Not only has the overall divorce rate risen—and particularly so since the 1960s—but so too have the divorce rates for men and women in each age group. For example, the divorce rate for married men aged 30 to 34 rose from about 4 per thousand in 1960 to about 28 per thousand in 1994—a sevenfold increase. In general, the increases have been proportionately greatest at the youngest age groups, and particularly for those in their twenties. Divorce rates rose fastest in the late 1960s and early 1970s; in contrast, during the 1980s and early 1990s, the increases were more modest, but nevertheless in general maintained a continuing upward path.

Divorces of Married Couples by Their Year of Marriage

A clearer and deeper insight into how divorce rates in successive years have a cumulative effect upon the marriages of different groups of couples can be gained by considering the proportions of marriages solemnised in selected years which have ended in divorce, by certain durations of marriage. Figure 9 (p. 42) provides such an analysis and indicates that the more recent the year of marriage, the greater the proportion of marriages which have ended in divorce by a given duration of marriage. For example, 3 per cent of couples who married in 1951 had divorced within 10 years; the corresponding proportions for those married in 1961, 1971 and 1981 were 7, 17, and 23 per cent, respectively. In addition, the proportions divorced within the early years of marriage have increased more rapidly for marriages in more recent years, than have the proportions divorced by longer durations. The dotted line in Figure 9 represents the proportion of recently married couples who would ultimately divorce, were the divorce rates observed in 1993/1994 to persist unchanged into the future. On this assumption, two in five marriages would ultimately end in divorce. A similar kind of calculation indicates that just over one in four children would experience divorce in their family before reaching age 16.

Recent divorce law has emphasised that the welfare of children must be paramount when marriages break down and parents make divorce arrangements. More generally, families containing children, and especially those containing *dependent* children, are of particular interest to legislators and those concerned with social policy. The remaining sections concentrate upon families,* and distinguish families containing one or more dependent children.**

The Effects of Recent Trends in Fertility, Marriage, Divorce and Cohabitation

One of the main results of the increase in the incidence of births taking place outside marriage has been a growth in the number of one-parent families headed by a single lone mother—that is, by a never-married mother—without a partner. In addition, the increase in separation and divorce has also led to growing numbers of separated and divorced lone-parent families.

Figure 10 (p. 43) illustrates the increase in the proportion of all families* with dependent children** which were one-parent families. The overall proportion grew steadily between 1971 and 1986; about one in 12 families was a one-parent family in 1971, whereas the proportion was one in seven in 1986. It may be seen that most of the increase in this period was due to a growth in divorced lone mothers, followed by a slightly smaller growth in single lone mothers.

After 1986, there was a more rapid increase in the proportion of all families with dependent children which were one-parent families—from one in seven in 1986 to between one in four and one in five in 1995. The fastest growth was in *single* lone mothers; the proportion they formed of all families with dependent children more than doubled in this period, from one in 30 to one in 12. The second largest growth was amongst separated lone mothers who, in 1995, accounted for over 1½ times the proportion they did in 1986. (Of course, a proportion of separated lone parents would have previously been living in cohabiting unions, rather than as married couples.) However, taken together, separated and divorced lone mothers formed one in eight of all

---

* A family is defined as either a married or cohabiting couple on their own, or with their never-married children (who have no children of their own), or lone parents with similar such children.

** A dependent child is aged either under 16, or from 16 to 18, inclusive, and in full-time education.

families with dependent children in 1995—just over one half of all one-parent families.

Figure 10 (p. 43) showed the proportion of all families with dependent children which were one-parent families; the majority of families with dependent children, albeit a diminishing majority, are, of course, married-couple families (and a small, but growing, proportion are cohabiting-couple families). In 1986 88 per cent of families with dependent children where the head of the family was aged under 60 were either married-couple families or cohabiting-couple families; by 1994 this proportion had fallen to 82 per cent—see Table 2. However, this overall decline conceals two contrasting trends; married-couple families accounted for 83 per cent of all families in 1986 but only 71 per cent in 1994—a fall of 12 per cent—whereas cohabiting-couple families formed five per cent of all families in 1986, but 11 per cent in 1994—an *increase* of six per cent.

However, on examining the separate trends for families with dependent children and those with non-dependent children only, it is clear that the proportions of those with dependent children changed more quickly than of those with non-dependent children only. For example, married-couple families with dependent children formed 49 per cent of all families in 1986, but only 42 per cent in 1994; in contrast married-couple families with non-dependent children only represented about the same proportion for most of the period. Similarly, the proportion of cohabiting couples with dependent children doubled, but the proportion with non-dependent children remained only fairly constant. A similar type of situation also occurred for lone-parent families. It is likely that a generational effect is the explanation; there has been much more of a decline in the proportion married—and an increase in the proportions cohabiting and being a lone parent—at the younger ages, those aged under 30, than at older ages, and it is the former group who are much more likely to have dependent children, and the latter group who are more likely to have non-dependent children.

Types of Families in Which Men and Women Live, According to Their Age

An enormous number of changes can occur to men and women in the types of families in which they live between the ages of 18 and 59. This age-range covers some of the most significant changes in the pattern of family living: leaving home, forming one's initial partnership; marriage or long-term union formation; having children, and, for some, separation, divorce, and lone parenthood, followed by children leaving home.

Table 2
Trends in Family Composition, All Families, 1986-94, Great Britain

Percentages

Type of family with head aged under 60	Year				
	1986	1988	1990	1992	1994
Married-couple families*	83	79	76	74	71
Cohabiting-couple families*	5	8	8	9	11
Lone-parent families+	12	13	16	16	18
Couple families with no children					
Married couples	22	22	22	21	21
Cohabiting couples	3	5	5	6	6
Couple families with dependent children					
Married couples	49	46	43	42	42
Cohabiting couples	2	3	3	3	4
Couple families with non-dependent children only					
Married couples	11	11	11	11	8
Cohabiting couples	0.3	0.3	0.4	0.3	0.2
Lone-parent families with dependent children					
Lone single mothers	2	3	4	5	5
Lone separated mothers	2	2	2	3	3
Lone divorced mothers	4	4	4	4	5
Lone widowed mothers	0.5	0.6	0.6	0.5	0.6
Lone fathers	0.8	0.8	0.8	1	1
Lone-parent families with non-dependent children only	3	3	4	3	3
All families* -percentage	100	100	100	100	100
-sample size	5003	4974	4740	4899	4621

* with or without children
+ with either dependent children, non-dependent children or both
Source: *General Household Survey*

Although overall the majority of men and women aged under 60 are husbands and wives, and although the majority of families are married-couple families, the profile of the different family types varies considerably by age of the head of the family as Figure 11a (p. 44) shows. (The head of the family is convention-ally taken as the husband or male partner in couple-families, and the lone parent in one-parent families.)

In the youngest age-group, where the family head is a teenager, three quarters of families are lone-mother families with depend-ent children. Figure 11b (p. 45) shows that the majority—almost nine in every ten— are single lone mothers. (It should be men-tioned that the *number* of families with a teenage head is compar-atively small—also that teenage lone mothers account for less than four per cent of all lone mothers.) Returning to Figure 11a, the proportion of lone-mother families with dependent children declines quite rapidly with increasing age of family head, such that amongst families where family heads are in their thirties, the proportion is only 18 per cent. Cohabiting-couple families without children are relatively more numerous than their married-couple counterparts where the man is in his teens or early twenties, but, at all older ages, the reverse is the case.

Figure 11a also shows that the proportion of married couples with dependent children increases from age 25 of the husband up to about age 40, after which the proportion of married couples with non-dependent children starts to grow, as does the propor-tion for married couples without any children living with them. Although Figure 11a is really a snapshot in the early 1990s of the profile of families with heads of different ages, it does give a rough picture of the evolution of families—just like individuals, their circumstances change with the passage of time. However, such an interpretation is really only valid when there has been a 'stationary situation' for at least one generation, that is, when marriage, divorce and birth rates have remained constant, as has also the level of cohabitation. In fact, as is clear from the above, there have been some important changes in the last decade alone.

Figure 11b gives a corresponding analysis of all lone parents. Single lone mothers form over eight in every ten lone-parent families amongst lone parents in their teens and amongst those in their early twenties, and separated and divorced lone mothers represent the majority of lone parents in their thirties and early forties. At older ages, however, lone parents with non-dependent children only make up an increasing part of the total. Over three quarters of lone parents aged 50 or over come into this category.

Trends in Household Composition

Until this point, discussion has centred upon families rather than upon households. Some of the developments mentioned above can be viewed in a broader context by considering how household composition has changed in recent decades. Table 3 shows the trends since 1961.

Table 3
Composition of households, by type of household and family, 1961-1994, Great Britain

Percentages

Type of household	1961	1971	1981	1991	1994
One-person households					
Under pensionable age	4	6	8	11	12
Over pensionable age	7	12	14	16	15
Two or more unrelated adults	5	4	5	3	3
*One-family households**					
Married couples with:					
no children	26	27	26	28	27
1-2 dependent children+	30	26	25	20	20
3 or more dependent children+	8	9	6	5	5
Non-dependent children only	10	8	8	8	6
Lone parent with:					
Dependent children+	2	3	5	6	7
Non-dependent children only	4	4	4	4	3
Two or more families	3	1	1	1	1
Number of households					
(=100%)(millions)	16.2	18.2	19.5	22.4	23.1

* these households may contain some individuals not members of the nuclear family
+ may also include non-dependent children
Source: Censuses, apart from General Household Survey for 1994 data

Multi-family households formed three per cent of all households in 1961 but have since declined to just below one per cent in 1994. During the 1970s and 1980s there was emphasis upon the provision of first public and then private housing which encouraged those in families—and those not in families—to acquire their own separate accommodation. There is evidence, too, that lone-parent families—who historically were more likely than other families to live in multi-family households—increasingly became one-family households throughout this period.

The trend towards people living alone has been particularly notable; since 1961, in relative numbers, one-person households have almost trebled for those under pensionable age, and more than doubled for those of pensionable age. In fact, the growth in living alone has been most marked amongst the most elderly—those aged 75 and over. One in three such elderly men were living alone in 1994, compared with only one in four in 1973. The majority, about six in every ten, of elderly women were living alone in 1994, compared with five in ten in 1973. The main reason for this change has been increased longevity, but better health and economic well-being, as well as a desire to remain independent as long as possible, have, no doubt, also played a part. It is also notable that one in ten men aged from 25 to 44 was living alone in 1994—three times the proportion in 1973—reflecting the decline in marriage and the rise in separation and divorce.

As a result of these trends, over one quarter of all households in Great Britain were one-person households in 1994. Related to this trend has been the decline in household-sharing between unrelated people; the proportion of such households almost halved between 1961 and 1994.

Single-family households consisting of a married-couple family and one or two dependent children have also declined considerably during the last 30 years or so; they formed three in every ten households in 1961, but only two in every ten in 1994. Similar families with three or more dependent children, and those with non-dependent children only, have also become rarer amongst all households. However, there has been a substantial growth in lone-parent households; one-family households consisting of lone parents with dependent children formed two per cent of all households in 1961, but seven per cent in 1994.

Conclusion

The changing patterns of fertility, marriage, divorce, cohabitation and of living alone have meant that family and household structures have become more diverse, and also that individuals are more likely to experience living in a greater variety of types of families and households during their lifetime. This tendency has been reinforced by the increase in longevity and in repartnering after the breakdown of marriage and informal unions. The pattern of parenthood has also changed; in general women are having fewer children and at older ages—and an increasing proportion are choosing not to have any children at all. In many respects, similar trends have been observed in most European countries. Possibly a common strand may be traced through many of the trends and characteristics described above—that of the growth of individualism, or the increasing exercise of choice. Of course, exercising choice, or the growing emphasis upon individual development and fulfilment, is much easier in a society if different patterns of demographic behaviour are generally accepted as valid alternatives, and the trend towards a variety of norms is perhaps the most significant of post-war social changes.

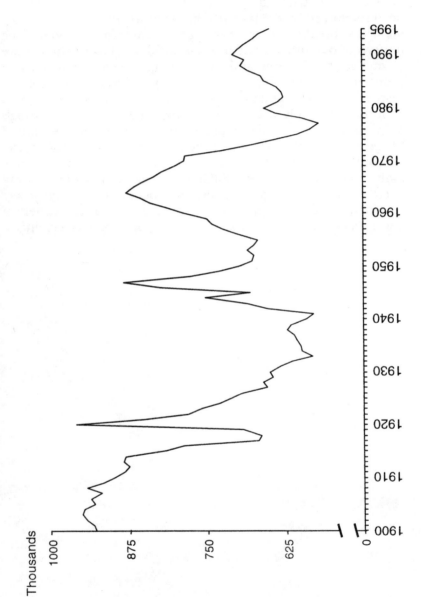

Figure 1 Live births, 1900-95, England and Wales

35

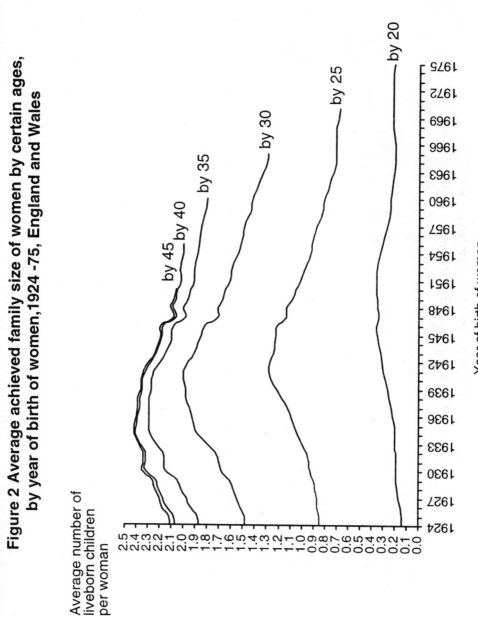

Figure 2 Average achieved family size of women by certain ages, by year of birth of women, 1924-75, England and Wales

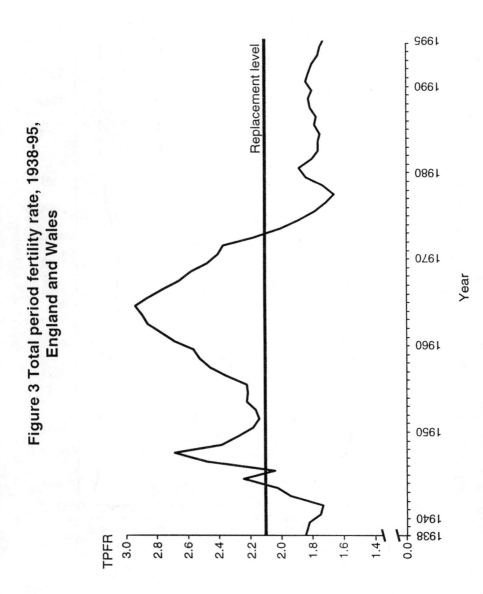

Figure 3 Total period fertility rate, 1938-95,
England and Wales

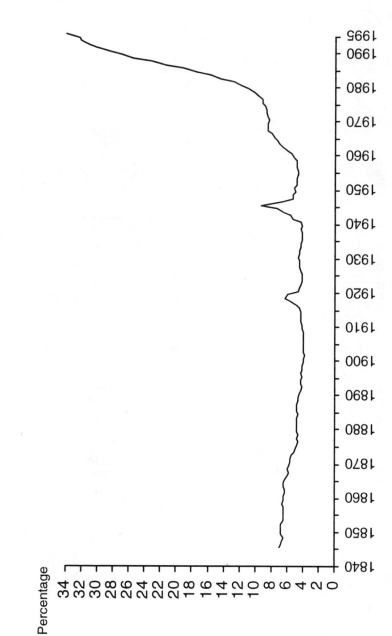

Figure 4 Births outside marriage as a percentage of all live births, 1845-1995, England and Wales

Figure 5 Live births outside marriage as a percentage of all live births, 1985-95, England and Wales

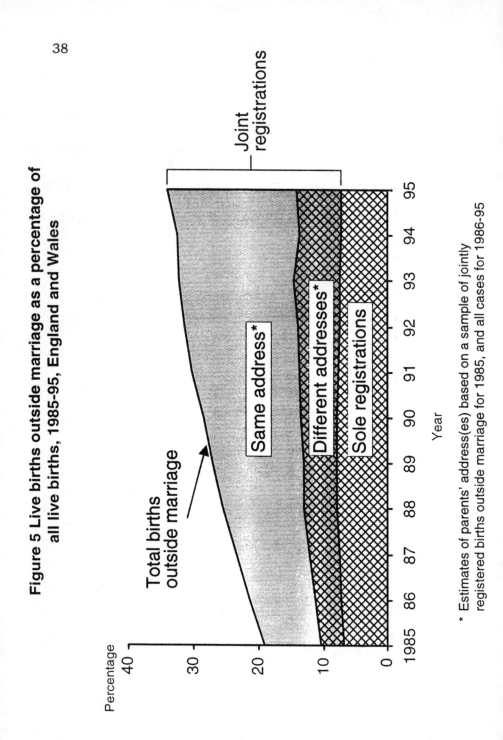

* Estimates of parents' address(es) based on a sample of jointly registered births outside marriage for 1985, and all cases for 1986-95

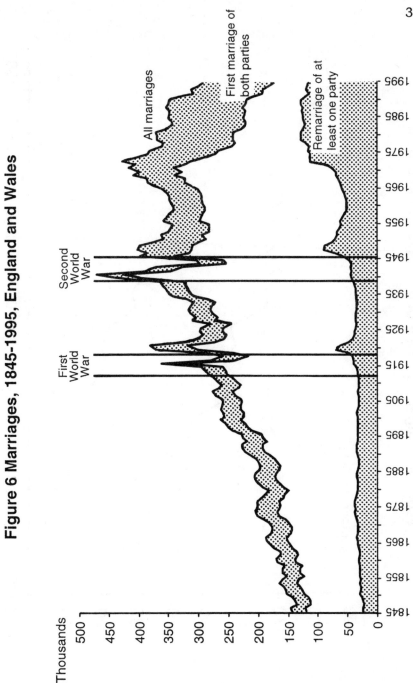

Figure 6 Marriages, 1845-1995, England and Wales

Figure 7 Percentages of women who reported that they had pre-maritally cohabited with their future husband for (a) all first marriages* and (b) all second marriages†, by year of marriage, Great Britain

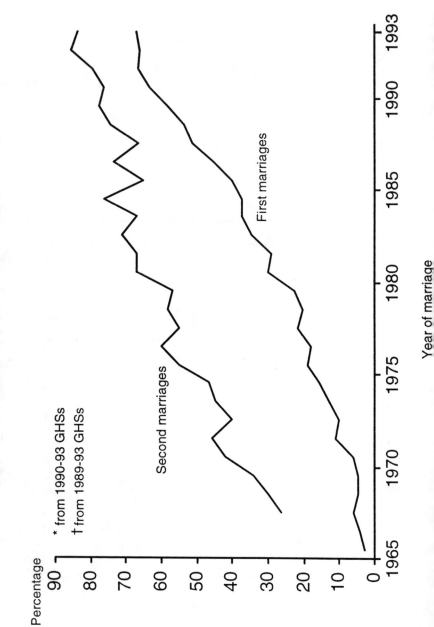

Percentage

* from 1990-93 GHSs
† from 1989-93 GHSs

First marriages

Second marriages

Year of marriage

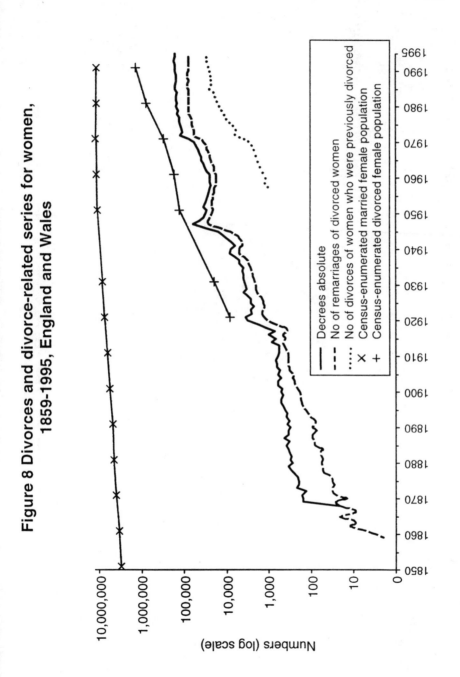

Figure 8 Divorces and divorce-related series for women, 1859-1995, England and Wales

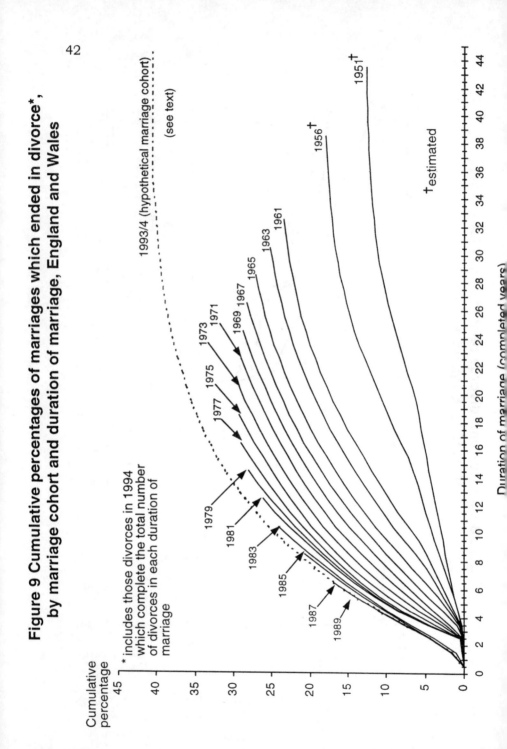

Figure 9 Cumulative percentages of marriages which ended in divorce*, by marriage cohort and duration of marriage, England and Wales

Cumulative percentage

* includes those divorces in 1994 which complete the total number of divorces in each duration of marriage

1993/4 (hypothetical marriage cohort)

(see text)

†estimated

Duration of marriage (completed years)

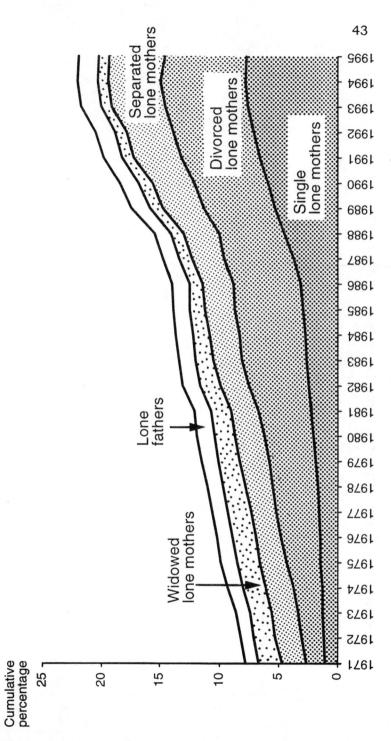

Figure 10 Percentages of all families with dependent children headed by lone mothers (by their marital status) and by lone fathers, 1971-95, Great Britain

44

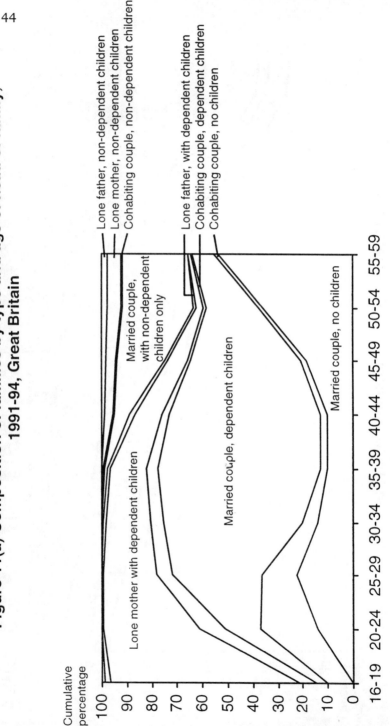

Figure 11(a) Composition of families by type and age of head of family, 1991-94, Great Britain

Cumulative percentage

Lone father, non-dependent children
Lone mother, non-dependent children
Cohabiting couple, non-dependent children

Lone father, with dependent children
Cohabiting couple, dependent children
Cohabiting couple, no children

Married couple, with non-dependent children only

Lone mother with dependent children

Married couple, dependent children

Married couple, no children

Age of head of family

16-19 20-24 25-29 30-34 35-39 40-44 45-49 50-54 55-59

Figure 11(b) Composition of one-parent families by type and age of parent, 1991-94, Great Britain

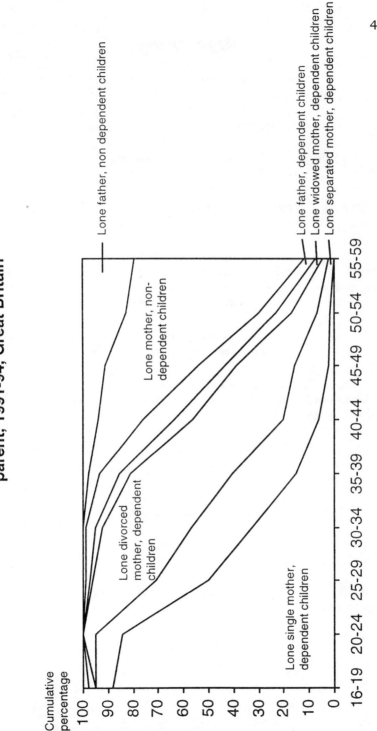

Cumulative percentage

Lone father, non dependent children

Lone mother, non-dependent children

Lone divorced mother, dependent children

Lone single mother, dependent children

Lone father, dependent children
Lone widowed mother, dependent children
Lone separated mother, dependent children

Age of parent

16-19 20-24 25-29 30-34 35-39 40-44 45-49 50-54 55-59

References

This chapter has drawn heavily from the following articles—particularly 'Families and households in Great Britain'—which have been published in *Population Trends*; the articles contain further references which provide further information and details.

Armitage, R. and Babb, P., 'Trends in fertility', *Population Trends*, Vol. 84, London: HMSO, 1996.

Haskey, J., 'Trends in marriage and divorce in England and Wales, 1837-1987', *Population Trends*, Vol. 48, London: HMSO, 1987.

Haskey, J., 'Trends in marriage and cohabitation: the decline in marriage and the changing pattern of living in partnerships', *Population Trends*, Vol. 80, London: HMSO, 1995.

Haskey, J., 'Families and households in Great Britain', *Population Trends*, Vol. 86, London: HMSO, 1996.

Haskey, J., 'The proportion of married couples who divorce: past patterns and current prospects', *Population Trends*, Vol. 83, London: HMSO, 1996.

Werner, B., 'Fertility statistics from birth registrations in England and Wales, 1837-1987', *Population Trends*, Vol. 48, London: HMSO, 1987.

For Further Reading:

Anderson, M., *Approaches to the History of the Western Family, 1500-1914*, London: Macmillan, 1980.

Houlbrooke, R., *The English Family 1450-1700*, London: Longman, 1992.

Laslett, P. and Wall, R. (eds.), *Household and Family in Past Time*, Cambridge: Cambridge University Press, 1972.

Laslett, P., *Family Life and Illicit Love in Earlier Generations: Essays in Historical Sociology*, Cambridge: Cambridge University Press, 1977.

Macfarlane, A., *Marriage and Love in England 1300-1840*, Oxford: Blackwell, 1986.

Newman, P. and Smith, A., *Social Focus on Families*, Office for National Statistics, London: The Stationery Office, 1997.

Office of Population Censuses and Surveys/General Register Office for Scotland, *1991 Census Household and Family Composition (10 per cent) Great Britain*, London: HMSO, 1994.

Office of Population Censuses and Surveys, *The Family (Papers presented to the British Society for Population Studies Conference at the University of Bath, 14-16 September 1983)*, Occasional Paper 31, OPCS, 1983.

Office of Population Censuses and Surveys, Social Survey Division, *Living in Britain: Results from the 1994 General Household Survey*, London: HMSO, 1996.

Stone, L., *The Family, Sex and Marriage in England 1500 -1800*, London: Weidenfeld and Nicolson, 1977.

Wrigley, A. and Schofield, R., *The Population History of England 1541-1871: A Reconstruction*, London: Edward Arnold, 1981.

Young, M. and Willmott, P., *Family and Kinship in East London*, London: Routledge and Kegan Paul, 1957.

Commentaries

Family Change: Issues and Implications

Kathleen Kiernan

Introduction

IN recent decades there has been a shift in family life from demographic and economic stability to demographic and economic diversity that has recast the relationship between the family and public policy.

At the outset it is important to emphasise the fact that currently the dominant family form in Britain continues to be the married couple, with whom children live until they grow up, and which ends when one of the spouses dies. However, as John Haskey's chapter shows, since the 1970s there have been some major changes in demographic behaviour that affect the ways that families are formed and end. People have been marrying later and divorcing more. They have also been cohabiting to a greater extent: as a prelude to marriage, instead of marrying, or between marriages. Lone-parent families have become more prevalent, arising from divorce, the break-up of cohabiting unions, and to a lesser extent from young women having children on their own. Partnerships between men and women have become more varied in type and fragile, whilst in recent times parenthood is being postponed, avoided by a growing minority, and occurring more often outside marriage.

Parallelling these demographic developments are economic ones that have profoundly affected family life. These include the marked increase in the level of women's participation in the labour market and the concomitant passing of the homemaker-mother and breadwinner-father division of labour, as well as the growth in insecure employment and unemployment.

Much of the post-war welfare state was founded on the premise of demographic stability and economic certainty. The 1950s was an era when death and divorce rates were both so low that the chances of children experiencing family dissolution were probably

51

at their lowest ever: death rates had been declining over the course of the twentieth century and divorce rates did not start to increase on a significant scale until the 1960s. Additionally, the 1950s and 1960s witnessed the climax of the specialisation between men and women in the two spheres of family and employment. Thereafter the speed of change in terms of more and more mothers participating in the labour market intensified with each passing decade. Here we examine these developments and consider their implications for the public and private domains of life.

Marriage and Cohabitation

Since around the beginning of the 1970s young people in Britain, as in most western European countries, have been marrying at increasingly older ages and fewer of them are marrying at all, a trend that continues to the present day. The sharp falls in marriage rates have been accompanied by a rise in the proportion of young people in cohabiting unions, and nowadays it has become almost the norm to cohabit before marrying. But cohabitation is not the whole story in the decline in marriage rates. Young people are also spending longer periods of time as solos than in the recent past; living with their parents, on their own or sharing with others. In fact young people's formal marriage behaviour in the 1990s is more reminiscent of the marriage patterns of their grandparents' or great-grandparents' than of their parents' generation.

Britain, like several other developed societies, may be going through a transition in the way that men and women become couples or partners. Drawing on the experience of the Swedish population, which is the nation that has gone furthest in these developments, a number of stages can be identified. Simplifying, in the first stage cohabitation emerges as a deviant or *avant garde* phenomenon practised by a small group of the population, whilst the great majority of the population marry directly. In the second stage cohabitation functions as either a prelude to marriage or a probationary period where the strength of the relationship is tested prior to committing to marriage and is predominantly a childless phase. In the third stage cohabitation becomes socially acceptable as an alternative to marriage and becoming a parent is no longer restricted to marriage. Finally, in the fourth stage, cohabitation and marriage become indistinguishable with children being born and reared within both, and the partnership transition could be said to be complete.[1] Sweden and Denmark are countries that have made the transition to this fourth stage. These stages may vary in duration, but once a society has reached a particular stage it is unlikely that there will be a return to an earlier stage. Also, once a certain stage has been reached all the previous types of cohabiting unions can co-exist. These stages identified at the societal level also have their parallels at the level of the individual. At any given time cohabitation may have different meanings for the men and women involved; for example, it may be viewed as an alternative to being single, or as a precursor to marriage, or as a substitute for marriage. How a couple perceives their cohabitation may change with the passage of time and may also vary between the partners.

Dissecting the cohabitation *process* in this way highlights the diversity of the phenomenon. Britain has certainly moved beyond stage one. Currently, the majority of cohabitation in this country is still the prelude type but, with the substantial growth in having children outside marriage that has occurred from the 1980s, there are increasing signs of movement to cohabitation as an alternative to marriage. If cohabitation is becoming more long-standing and children are increasingly being not only born but being reared throughout their childhood in such unions, then public and private institutions will need to address the implications of this novel development. The interesting question is how legal institutions will accommodate themselves to the debate that, in the simplest terms, could be said to have two main points of view. One argues that the legal distinction between marriage and cohabitation should be maintained as its removal would undermine the position of marriage, whilst another would be reluctant to give cohabitation full recognition on the grounds that it forces upon unmarried couples a legal framework which, by the act of cohabiting, they may be trying to avoid. A similar debate raged in Sweden in the early 1970s and is still not fully resolved.[2] Sweden is the country where cohabitation has been most long-standing and is most prevalent, but even here there is a reluctance to accord the same rights to cohabitants and married couples. Generally, it would seem that countries with longer experiences of the cohabitation issue have tended to opt for legislative solutions that compensate cohabitants for drawbacks arising from being outside the legal framework, but mainly on an *ad hoc* basis.

Becoming a Parent

The three major and recent themes in the transition to parenthood in Britain and other European societies are later entry into parenthood, lower probabilities of parenthood and greater probabilities of having a child outside marriage. Across most European countries in recent decades there has been a movement to later entry into motherhood. Information on becoming a father is rare but we assume that trends have followed the same general direction as that seen for motherhood.

Changing fertility patterns have short- and long-term effects. Significant shifts to an older age-pattern of childbearing has implications for the obstetric and gynaecological services as women having their first child in their thirties, others things being equal, require more medical resources. On the other hand, they will have contributed more taxes and national insurance contributions prior to becoming mothers than women who become mothers at a younger age. Changes in the timing of childbearing and declines in fertility affect the planning of hospitals, schools and the housing market. Fertility patterns are also the main engine driving the age distribution of the population. Declining fertility leads to an ageing of the population and to a decline in the ratio of working-age population to the elderly population with ensuing implications for the funding of pensions and health care. Moreover, if an increased proportion of the social welfare budget needed to be allocated to the elderly this could reduce the resources available to other groups including children, lone-parent families and the unemployed.

A later start to parenthood may be driven by both positive and negative impetuses. A later start allows young people to acquire more educational and occupational training as well as higher savings and incomes. Additionally, later marriage and parenthood are associated with lower risks of marital breakdown and later motherhood is also associated with a greater attachment to the labour market which, in the event of divorce, may lessen the deprivations that are a frequent accompaniment to divorce. On the other hand, in an era of rising expectations couples may be postponing having children because raising children is expensive, and many families may feel that they need two employed adults to provide a decent standard of living for themselves and their children. Moreover, women have become increasingly committed to being in the labour market and leaving the labour force for extended periods has become less popular. Faced with such dilemmas and economic stresses, including uncertain job prospects and low incomes, some couples may postpone having children to later than they would ideally wish, and have fewer children or none at all.

Another major and recent feature of family demography which is intimately related to developments in cohabitation is the increased separation of marriage and childbearing. In Britain and other northern and western European countries there has been a noticeable increase in the proportions of births outside marriage, and in many of these countries extra-marital births are now making a significant contribution to the overall level of fertility. In Britain the proportion of all births occurring outside marriage in 1995 was 34 per cent, up from eight per cent in 1971 and 13 per cent in 1981. In 1995 six out of ten of these children were jointly registered by both parents who were living at the same address at the time of the birth. Much of the growth in extra-marital childbearing emanates from cohabiting couples, whilst the propensity for women to have a baby on their own has not shown as marked a change over recent decades.

The rise of childbearing within cohabiting unions and the creation of families outside legal marriage raise a number of issues. A major one is to what extent cohabiting unions and marriages are similar and to what extent are they different? How, if at all, do they differ with respect to responsibilities for partners and children, pooling of resources, the division of labour within the household and labour market, etc?

Evidence is accruing which suggests that there are some differences between marital and cohabiting unions. For example, cohabiting unions are less stable and when these unions break up fathers of children born outside marriage may be less involved with their children on dimensions such as paying child support, visiting their children, and being involved in child rearing decisions than are fathers whose children were born within marriage. Never-married cohabiting couples with children are also amongst the poorest families in Britain, suggesting that cohabiting unions may be a response to socio-economic disadvantage as well as a response to progressive developments such as higher expectations of relationships and marriage, greater female autonomy etc.

Divorce Trends

Alongside the increasing separation of marriage and childbearing there has also been, with the rise in divorce, the increasing separation of childbearing and child rearing for at least one of the parents, typically the father. It remains the case that death terminates the majority of marriages. However, marriages are increasingly being dissolved by divorce at a stage in marriage before death has made any significant inroad, and at a stage in the marriage when there are likely to be dependent children. Britain has one of the highest divorce rates in Europe with almost one in four recent marriages having dissolved by the tenth wedding anniversary. If recent divorce rates were to continue it is estimated that in most countries in Europe the chances of couples divorcing would be around one in three: with Sweden, Denmark, and the United Kingdom highest at around two out of five and some of the southern European countries lagging behind at one in ten or less.[3] With the rise of cohabitation the issue of the dissolution of unions is becoming more complex as the true number of separations is not captured in official statistics on legal separations or divorce.

Amongst children born since the 1970s over 20 per cent have experienced the dissolution of their parents' marriage by the time they are age 16, compared with less than 10 per cent of children born in the 1960s or earlier. As marriages are tending to break up sooner, more couples are likely to be childless but, amongst couples with children, the children are likely to be younger and thus exposed to spending longer periods of time in lone-parent families. As a consequence of divorce there has been a growth in lone-parent families, the residential separation of fathers from their children, remarried couples, and step-families.

Effects of Divorce

Divorce is perhaps one of the most significant social developments of recent decades and one of the major unresolved social issues that brings to the fore fundamental issues about the roles of men and women in society and the care of and support for children. For example, take the case of divorce legislation. Divorce legislation in many countries has been increasingly moving to the 'clean-break principle', placing greater emphasis on the desirability of the partners being self-sufficient so far as is possible after the divorce. However, changes which promote post-divorce financial independence reflect back upon arrangements within marriage, and imply that both spouses should be prudent and maintain their market potential throughout marriage in case divorce should occur. But this is difficult if the couple become parents.

There can be opportunity costs to being born a female, but there are more so to becoming a mother, and whilst some argue that women's disadvantages are structural to society and husbands should not bear the costs in event of divorce, others have argued that the disadvantages that women face because of having children by their husband should be perhaps compensated for by him. Moreover, the foregone earnings of mothers who take time out of the labour market to care for their children could be seen just as much as part of the cost of rearing the next generation of citizens and workers as the money that is directly spent on children. The bearing and rearing of children undoubtedly reduces women's economic power, which in turn leads to other economic consequences, such as lack of adequate personal pension rights.

The division of pensions, or 'pension splitting' on divorce or at the point of retirement, is increasingly the subject of discussion and debate which arises because typically both spouses have not acquired comparable pension entitlements due to, in the majority of cases, the mother having taken time out of the labour market to care for children. The question of what claims, if any, ex-wives should have on a former spouse's occupational pension rights and how and when they should be divided is an important social policy issue.

A substantial proportion of divorced persons eventually remarry. Men are more likely than women to remarry and are also likely to remarry more quickly after a divorce. Divorced men, as well as being more likely to remarry, are also more likely to cohabit than are divorced women. Re-partnering for men raises the issue as to whether they will have adequate resources to support two families, and, if this is not possible, which of these families will have recourse to state support. The answer has frequently been that the first family tends to have to rely on state support in the absence of other adequate sources of income.

However this is changing, particularly since the advent of the Child Support Agency with the emphasis increasingly being put on the responsibilities of biological fatherhood as opposed to social fatherhood.

Lone-parent Families

The great majority of lone-parent families are lone-mother families for which there are three main causes. The major one is partnership breakdown; either formal partnerships contracted through marriage or informal ones formed by cohabitation. The death of a father was a prominent cause of lone motherhood as late as the 1960s, but nowadays is a minor cause. Most of the remainder of lone-mother families consist of never-married mothers rearing their children on their own.

The available broad evidence suggests that over one-half of lone parents leave this status within five years, through re-marriage, children leaving home or children attaining ages when they are no longer classified as children.[4] This may seem a short time in the lives of adults, but for children five years is a significant part of childhood.

The growth in lone-mother families, up from 11 per cent of all families with dependent children in 1981 to 21 per cent in 1994, and the postponement of parenthood discussed earlier, are not unconnected. The number of lone mothers in a population depends on two main factors: the total number of women of childbearing age in the population and the proportion of these that become lone parents. Increases in the proportion of children with lone parents occur if either the number of children in lone-parent families goes up or if the number of children in two-parent families goes down. Over the last decade both these changes have occurred and both have contributed to the increase in the proportion of children being reared in lone-parent families. The reduction in married-couple families with children has in effect magnified the increase in the lone parent population and the proportion of children living in lone-parent families.

Both developments might suggest a society that is lacking in its support of families with children, with declining marriage and fertility rates indicating a society that is not organised around or concerned with families and children, and the increasing proportion of lone-parent families indicating conditions in which it is difficult to hold families together.

Being reared by a lone parent is frequently not a long-term arrangement as a substantial proportion of divorced persons eventually remarry. Remarriages are also at greater risk of dissolving than are first marriages. We do not know whether different types of reconstituted and blended families have greater risks of breaking up but there is some information from the United States which suggests that the risks increase with the complexity of the re-formed families.[5] For example, couples in which only one of the parties has been previously married and where there are no step-children have the lowest risk, whilst those marriages where both husband and wife are remarrying and where there are step-children have the highest risk.

Children in Families

As a consequence of these demographic changes children are increasingly experiencing a variety of family settings as they pass through childhood and adolescence. The implications of these changing circumstances for the welfare and development of children both in the short and the more long term have yet to be fully assessed. However, there is a good deal of evidence that children who experience the break-up of their parents' marriage or union are more likely to experience poverty or reduced economic circumstances than children who grow up with both natural parents. The financial exigencies associated with marital breakdown arise from the precarious economic position of lone mothers, with whom most children reside, and the dis-economies of scale associated with the maintenance of two households, when fathers live apart from their children. The low incomes of lone-mother families are due to a combination of factors: low earnings from employment, lack of or low levels of child support from the natural father, meagre or inadequate state support. Even children from relatively advantaged backgrounds experience a loss of economic resources when their parents live apart. In Britain in the 1990s around 80 per cent of lone mothers rely on state benefits to support themselves and their children. Such limited finances may affect a child's school attainment in that many lone mothers may not be able to afford the toys, books, sports equipment, home computers and other goods that can aid school success. Limited income may also mean that lone-mother families are more likely to be living in areas with poorer quality schools. Moreover, children living with lone mothers may leave school early to seek employment to assist with the family finances or even work long hours whilst still at school to compensate for lack of family finances to fund their own needs and social activities. Low educational attainment and early entry into the labour market in turn increase the likelihood of low occupational attainment, low incomes, unemployment and state dependency.

Divorce is also associated with a decline in the quantity and quality of contact between children and their non-residential parent, in the main their father, and the mothers may also be constrained in the time and energy they can devote to their children, particularly if they have to take on paid employment or increase their hours of work. Reductions in parental resources, such as the amount of attention, supervision and support they can give to their children, may increase the likelihood of academic failure and behaviour problems. The loss of parental role models may also reduce the learning of social skills required for the successful management of occupational and marital roles in later life.

Alongside these economic and sociological explanations are those from the psychological literature based on the concept of family stress which views divorce as a major strain for children. Many studies have shown that parental conflict prior to and during separation and post-separation can have a negative impact on children's psychological well-being.[6] Accompaniments to divorce such as moving house, changing schools, and loss of contact with paternal grandparents and other kin are also stressful for children. Nevertheless, children vary in their responses to stress and adversity: some children may be harmed and carry the legacy into adulthood, others may be more resilient, whilst others may show initial difficulties and subsequently adjust and recover.[7]

One of the challenges in assessing the legacy of divorce is being able to sort out the conditions that lead couples to separate and the potential effects on children from the consequences of the dissolution itself. Divorce is more likely to occur among couples with personal, social and economic problems. Thus the non-random nature of the divorcing population implies that the effects of factors that existed prior to the divorce, for example poverty, could be confused with its consequences. The selective nature of the population of children who experience parental divorce may lead to an over-stated impression of the effects of divorce by conflating pre-existing differences amongst children from disrupted families as compared with those from non-disrupted ones, with the fall-out from marital dissolution.

Undoubtedly, children benefit from being raised in an emotionally and economically secure two-parent family but, if this is not possible, the evidence from recent research suggests that in the context of the long-term welfare of children we should be as concerned about the conditions that precede divorce and sometimes lead to divorce, such as poverty and economic uncertainty, as we are with the consequences of marital break-up.[8]

Remarriage

Improvements in the economic well-being of lone mothers and their children have been remarkably dependent on remarriage. Lone mothers who marry or remarry boost their income level and are also the group most likely to move out of poverty. However, with the growth in cohabitation and unemployment, the benefits of re-partnering have become more subtle. It has been observed by Reuben Ford and colleagues[9] that entering a new partnership is not necessarily 'a passport to prosperity'. In many cases, particularly when the new union is a cohabitation rather than a marriage, it is often the start of further economic difficulties as such partnerships tend to be more fragile, with some new partners not staying very long. The group of lone mothers most likely to prosper in a new partnership are those who are employed and whose new partner is also in employment. The best route out of hardship for all families is undoubtedly to have both partners in employment.

Work and Family Life

Family well-being is remarkably dependent on an economy in which families can earn an adequate income from work. Employment is the main source of economic support for families and plays a pivotal role in the lives of both men and women. However, work can also constrain family life by limiting the time available for family tasks and interaction between family members, and conversely the obligations and responsibilities of family life may act as a constraint on labour force participation. Moreover, competing pressures of work and family obligations may make for inefficiencies both in parenting and employment.

Nowadays, most mothers are employed outside the home, a long-term trend that is unlikely to go into reverse or be reversible. Whether a mother continues in paid work or returns to the labour market after time out to care for children partly depends on the balance between the income that employment brings and the financial costs of childcare. The decision of a mother to work also depends on social and psychic costs and benefits related to her own needs, the needs of her children and the needs of the family unit. For a lone mother with no alternative source of income, the financial factor may be of critical importance.

Research on the effects of maternal employment on children has largely examined the impact on children's academic performance and achievements. The findings in relation to this issue tend to be ambiguous, contradictory and weak. There is as yet no robust evidence that maternal employment negatively or positively affects a child's educational achievement. In the USA, this is currently the subject of a major research initiative funded by the National Institute of Child Health and Development.[10] Early findings are that the amount of childcare was unrelated to children's cognitive and language development over the first three years of life but the quality of the childcare was an important factor.

Recognising that the worlds of work and family are interdependent implies the fostering and development of policies that ease the tensions between the two domains. Such policies are well rehearsed and include: maternity and parental leave; flexible hours of work including part-time employment; family leave to care for sick children; affordable quality childcare, including the provision of nursery schools and after-school care; tax concessions and child benefits and allowances. These policies directly and explicitly support families with children and give recognition to some of the costs in rearing the next generation.

The growth in women's employment is probably altering the economic arrangements between men and women. Women may increasingly be taking a greater share of the economic support of the household and men's prime responsibility is likely to have lessened. The proportion of women who depend on men and their degree of dependence may well decline further in the future, as women acquire more education, make more inroads into a wider range of occupations, progress up the occupational and political hierarchies and take less time out of the labour market to care for young children. Until men and women become financially autonomous, public policies will have to live with the legacy of existing regimes in which marriage both fostered financial dependency but also offered financial protection for women and children.

In recent years the growth in the labour force participation of married women with children, and increasingly young children, a trend that—other things being equal—is unlikely to go into reverse, has reduced the extent to which mothers are available to organise and support the home and care for family members. As a consequence, the tension between family and work may have become more severe. Moreover, such difficulties may be one of the important engines behind the growth in childlessness, delayed childbearing and reductions in fertility levels that have occurred in Britain and across Europe in recent decades. The psychic costs of combining work and caring for young children may lie behind some illuminating findings from the 1990 Eurobarometer Survey. Results from this survey suggest that if women and men in the Community at large were given a completely free choice, about eight out of ten women and four out of ten men would prefer *not* to work full-time when their children were under school-age.[11]

The modern family is, and is increasingly likely to be, headed by two workers rather than one. Female economic activity rates have increased and are likely to increase further. Today's young women have aspirations in terms of paid work and future employment patterns which threaten traditional public policy assumptions about a 'woman's place' and her 'natural role' in relation to home and care and which make the reconciliation of family and occupational careers all the more urgent.

Conclusion

The changing demography of families, together with the rise of dual-worker families and families with no workers, and an ageing population, speak to the co-ordination of a range of policies including social welfare policies, childcare, educational and training and employment policies, that support and develop families in a changing social and economic climate. The increased diversity and turnover in family life which largely emanates from partnership changes makes policy built on marriage increasingly problematic and suggests that parenthood rather than marriage should be the primary policy focus, and that parenthood rather than marriage contracts should underpin family relations.

An Endangered Species?

Patricia Morgan

Introduction

THE future of any society depends upon its ability to reproduce itself physically, socially and culturally, and its fortunes upon the qualities of the next generation. Such basic facts of life tend to be those most likely to be overlooked, perhaps because they are too close. Suppose the anthropological observer in us finds that tribe X has had a birthrate well below population replacement level for an unprecedented length of time. In scarcely more than a decade, the child population will be smaller than the elderly population. Proportionally more of the declining numbers of children are being born and reared in conditions where they are more likely to be under-resourced, socially if not materially, and which enhance all known risks to development. The fall in the birthrate is entirely accounted for by the decline of births within marriage, while lone mothers' family size is increasing.

As well as the women having progressively fewer children, or none at all, the marriage rate has fallen to an historical low. These marriages are breaking up at an exponential rate as each successive age-group divorces faster and more often than the one before. The decline in marriage and rise in age at marriage ought to be associated with higher marriage stability, but this has not occurred. Moreover, relationships are more prone to disintegrate before they get on the register, as cohabitation as a prelude to marriage increasingly gives way to cohabitation as a prelude to separation.[1] A result is that a growing proportion of men and women are not living with anybody, as families fall in numbers, grow smaller in size and shorter in life-span, and the fewer children are increasingly products of fatherlessness, broken or fragile relationships. On the face of it, is it easy to be optimistic about tribe X?

65

Post-modern Optimism

In our own past, even the prospect of developments so threatening to the cohesion of society and its capacity to replace itself adequately would probably have caused no small consternation and triggered remedial action. The will and the resources would have been marshalled to protect families and children as *the* social priority group, since they were the repositories of a cherished way of life, whose welfare was central to national identity and interests. However it is difficult now to find any recognition of the social functions of marriage, or its role in the cultural reproduction of populations and societies. Even more remarkable than the present scale of family fragmentation is the insistence that nothing significant or untoward is happening. There is even apparently cause for 'post-modern optimism' and something innovative to celebrate, as people 'shift away from the restrictive confines of normative roles and towards more equitable family relationships, with new conceptions of gender roles and a plurality of family forms'.[2] As David Popenhoe observes: 'For ideological reasons, even though the empirical data to support the trend are now overwhelming, the notion of "family decline" remains steeped in controversy',[3] and is still not intellectually respectable. Expressed concern about the health of the family is equated with undesirable political perspectives, even patriarchal plots to keep women subordinated, or insults to 'gay couples'.[4]

John Haskey's review simply reinforces the establishment position that family decline is a myth. There is evolution, not dissolution, where the 'changing patterns of fertility, marriage, divorce, cohabitation and of living alone' mean no more than that 'family and household structures have become more diverse, and also that individuals are more likely to experience living in a greater variety of types of families and households during their lifetime' (pp. 32-33). As the definition of family is stretched to cover any household, where any living situation and all transitional states are equally 'families', there is nothing to decline or dissolve, only movement between ever-transmuting 'family forms'.

The Authorised Version

This authorised account of demographic trends is clearly limited when it comes to describing and explaining change. Can it be said that 'families are under stress with the incidence of marital breakdown having grown considerably in the last generation', if this is just the way that 'the diversity of family forms has increased in recent decades' (p. 9)? Who are these particular 'families' which might come under stress and break down? The lack of any reference points also obviates any discussion of the effects. If the family is just a series of shifting forms, then claims that it is 'arguably the most important institution we have' and the 'well-attested framework in which to bring up children', say little more than that children are better off outside of residential care.

These multifarious new 'family forms' are treated simply as personal choices, or inventions, or 'lifestyle decisions'. No room here for that great staple of sociological and historical explanation—unintended consequences—or untidy mismatches and conflicts of means and ends. Supposedly, what people want and what they value are one with what they get. Haskey explains how:

> exercising choice, or ...individual development and fulfilment is much easier in a society if different patterns of demographic behaviour are generally accepted as valid alternatives, and the trend towards a variety of norms is perhaps the most significant of post-war social changes (p. 33).

This is the point at which an *is*, or a *will be*, tends to slip into an *ought*, and we find standards read off from the direction of trends, which we must embrace and facilitate for no other reason than that they are happening. Most children are still with their original two parents. But since it is the 'direction of future norms' that counts, two researchers speak of a 'policy framework that responds to the current realities of family life' [*sic*] as one 'which recognises that increasingly children will be brought up in "non-traditional" family forms'.[5]

The present discourse on the family is the product of profound hostility. As the argument now runs, marriage must be eliminated as a defining characteristic for analysis or social policy in order not to discriminate against its 'valid alternatives'. Indeed, *ad hoc* cohabitation and reproduction—or the 'fact of parenthood'—are meant to somehow take over as the recognised basis of family life to allow for fullest expression of that infinite 'diversity of family forms'. How family ties and parental obligations are supposed to emerge without 'institutional formality', or simply as emanations from the individuals' living arrangements or personal relations, is a mystery and it is painful to watch the exponents flounder in their own contradictions.[6] The all too obvious parallel is with those old Marxist exhortations to simply 'confront the possibility' of a classless society which achieves 'genuine consensus' while abnegating all norms.

A 'New Social Order' or Just Second-best?

It often sounds as if people's various living arrangements which do not conform to the norm of the two-parent family are the result of some kind of decision to create a new social order. However, where we end up is not necessarily the place we aimed to be. Outcomes may not represent the 'first-best' choice of the people involved. If anything, there is a growing gap between outcomes and aspirations for family life. Because there has been a shift in attitudes towards tolerating or permitting previously proscribed behaviour, this does not mean that people at large regard divorce, homosexuality, staying single or childless as desirable goals. Fewer than ever before may believe that such arrangements are morally wrong, but that is not to say that most think that marriage is outmoded, or being childless is ideal (in 1989 fewer than five per cent of European Union citizens took this view). The consistent return from opinion samples is that 90 per cent of young people want to marry and most want children. It is significant that respondents from Britain and Denmark, the countries with the highest divorce rates in Europe, were the most likely (at two out of three) to put relationship stability at the top of their list as an influence on the number of children.[7]

Failure to attain conventional goals, rather than the eager embrace of 'alternatives', is perhaps reflected in the way that married-couple families fell 12 per cent between 1986 and 1994, while cohabiting couples with children increased by six per cent, just as births within marriage are declining at double the rate they are rising outside. Just as the contraction of the family is faster than the advance of the 'alternatives', so, by the same token, it also reflects the way in which ideals have ceased to be imperatives, with a weakening of familism as a cultural value. Most may want marriage and children, but fewer believe it is right to stay together for the children, or important to have children, or even to be married.

Haskey draws a parallel with the fall in fertility and marriage rates in the 1930s, when there was a 'severe economic situation and widespread unemployment' (p. 14), and where '[t]he peaks and troughs around the time of the Depression and the two world wars are understandable given the prevailing circumstances' (p. 21). But in the 1930s, nobody was talking about the delay and decline in births and marriages, or more single people and childless couples, in terms of 'a diversity of family forms'.

Practical difficulties—uncertain job prospects and low incomes —everywhere cause marriages and births to be postponed and relinquished. The presence of children in the poverty statistics has swelled as their overall numbers in the population have declined, as those with children have become prone to spells of economic distress of a greater or lesser duration over the last two decades. The recent *Social Focus on Families*, which brings together national statistics on families in the UK, might well report how 'parents identified a lack of money as a key impact of having children'.[8] It contrasted their living standards with couples with no children who, as well as being the biggest spenders, occupied 'accommodation well above the standard; almost six in ten of these families [*sic*] lived in homes that were considered to be under-occupied'.[9] Children compete for limited parental resources of time, energy and money, while it is increasingly comfortable and immediately gratifying to be 'childfree'. This competition is intensified as the level of parental investment required to 'meet society's needs for productive workers and engaged citizens has gradually increased' along with desirable goods and services.

Children not only involve substantial extra costs but, since living standards, including mortgage commitments, are increasingly based on a two-income strategy, they also represent income foregone. With the collapse of family policy, the tax burden has been deposited on families, with those on lower incomes or with one main earner the hardest hit. In the circumstances, the criteria for responsible parenthood—establishing a home, having a decent margin against subsistence, and a parent available to provide sensitive care—are immensely contraceptive. Moreover, with increasing divorce, couples deciding whether to become parents are faced with uncertainty about the stability of their relationship as much as their economic security. In a 1993 survey, one in two European non-parents over 25 years of age put 'stability of the couple's relationships' at the top of the list of factors that might influence the number of children, followed by housing, unemployment and other economic problems. Yet, while the incentives to stay childless have increased considerably since the 1960s: 'few people take a conscious and immutable decision to remain childless; rather childlessness is often the outcome of a series of decisions not to have a child at the present time'.[10]

However, the economic circumstances which may lead people to forego marriage and induce childlessness may be insufficient to explain present increases in non-marital childbearing—which is higher on the lower rungs of the social ladder. A long line of demographic and ethnographic research links male employment and earnings to family formation and marital stability, but these must now be seen in interaction with differential welfare provision for married and lone parents, and the advent of housing and assistance programmes supporting broken families. While children may have become increasingly incompatible with marriage, it has become easier to support them outside. With the shift from one location, or welfare system, to another, the result is dual fertility markets, as marital and non-marital fertility diverge. The missing side of an explanatory triangle is likely to be accounted for by the 'technology shock', where Old Adam has been the beneficiary of easily available contraception and abortion. Ironically, women's ability to 'control' their fertility not only knocked the bottom out of taboos on pre-marital sex, but men's moral obligation to marry their pregnant girlfriend. If men no longer have to assume parental responsibility to engage in sexual relations, the women can marry the state instead—something with greatest appeal to those whose own personal economic, as well as marital, options are limited.

New Family Forms?

The truth is that childless couples, single people living alone, or those living together, with or without the intention to marry, are not treating themselves to new family forms or a 'greater variety of family structures'. They are what they have always been, and not 'such that we have to change our family definitions'.[11] Marital breakdown, putative fathers and unwed births have occurred whatever sort of family is regarded as the norm in a society. The only difference is that today's 'new family forms' are yesterday's immoralities. Fragmentation of any family system is likely to leave mother-child dyads in its wake, given the facts of mammalian reproduction. Family systems vary from society to society, but they are elaborately structured by morality, law, convention and economy. The characteristic of many of the living arrangements which are now elevated to the status of 'family forms' is precisely their lack of permanence and structure. This makes the fission in the nucleus of the family of a different order from other historical changes that, for example, might have involved a trend away from extended families, or towards small families, or from polygamy to monogamy.[12]

Despite attempts to find cultural precedents for the institutionalisation of the lone-mother unit, marriage is an age-old and universal framework for the ordering and understanding of family organisation, parental perspectives and behaviour, which creates obligations between the adult parties, their kin, and the couple and their children. As Blackstone remarked in 1775, in his commentaries on the law: 'the main end and design of marriage... being to ascertain and fix upon some certain person, to whom the care, the protection, the maintenance, and the education of the children should belong'.[13] The 'certain person' was a man. For women, biological and social parenthood invariably coincide. For men, there is a gap which is closed by marriage, where the 'necessity of imposing the bond of marriage' is 'practically and theoretically due to the fact that a father has to be made to look after his children'.[14]

What we are witnessing now is not the formalisation of other 'family structures', but the de-regulation of the conjugal nuclear family which we have known for centuries. Mavis Maclean and John Eekelaar in *The Parental Obligation* go so far as to talk of the 'collapse of marriage as the central organising institution of legal, familial relationships', as social programmes treat family members as individuals, and family law has relinquished most of its overt attempts to promote any particular ideas about family life. To this might be added the way in which provisions for families are now understood and developed with almost exclusive reference to lone parents, as the care and support of children has lost recognition when performed in the context of the two-parent family. The watershed was the advent of no-fault divorce, undermining marriage as a life-long commitment. At least Maclean and Eekelaar implicitly acknowledge that it is élites who have set the people free 'to move more easily into and out of what is becoming an essentially private arrangement'.[15]

However, it is one thing to say that marriage has been made something which may be now 'entered or left, as a matter of individual choice', and another to claim that it has become nothing but 'a subjective experience', in 'the private domain'.[16] To those involved, and the world at large, the 'piece of paper' still indicates a publicly expressed commitment and symbolic change in status. (When respondents to the British Household Panel Survey were asked about important events that had happened to themselves or their families over a year, one per cent mentioned a cohabitation, while nearly 20 per cent mentioned a wedding or engagement.)[17]

Liberalised divorce certainly alters the nature of the contract it terminates. Lacking the power to bind future behaviour, the incentive to invest resources in a relationship is undermined. But it is simplistic, as much as opportunist, to believe that—having rubbed out the prescriptive content from family law—divorce reform also abolished, at a stroke, the meaning and significance of marriage as an organising factor and reference point in people's lives and any influence this might have upon attitudes and behaviour. Assuredly, Maclean and Eekelaar recognise that while marriage may have been rendered legally 'empty', it might still remain, even if attenuated, a context for parenthood. But as they are also out to show that it has no behavioural consequences for the rearing of children, and is therefore defunct as a framework for family obligations, we are meant to ask with Brenda Hoggett, Law Commissioner, whether 'we should be considering whether the legal institution of marriage continues to serve any useful purpose'.[18]

This is the latest variation on the way in which dominant opinion has been running ahead of the statistics in its eagerness to announce the demise of the family. According to Reuben Ford and Jane Millar for the Rowntree Foundation, everyone has already embraced 'alternatives' to such an extent that lone parenthood is 'coming to be seen as another stage in the family life cycle'.[19] What has been repeated *ad nauseam* is that only a tiny, unrepresentative minority now lives in the conjugal, nuclear family, or even that this exists only on cornflake packets or in the imaginations of those set upon projecting a nostalgic ideal onto the real world. However, even if they are a shrinking majority, married-couple families still accounted for 71 per cent of those with dependent children in 1994. But, if the form cannot be denied, the next move is to void it of substance, by presenting marriage as meaningless and inconsequential. Cohabitees, who make up 11 per cent of those with children, can then pass into the lead as the expression of 'the new model' and 'emerging alternative ground' on which to base family relationships, which is 'outgrowing marriage in importance'.[20]

The Inescapable Data

Can we really take it as read that marriage now serves no useful purpose, whether in terms of the outcomes for children or the consequences for society? Is there no reason to suspect that the accelerating decay of the family unit represents a deterioration in the conditions of childhood, a rise in social and economic costs, even a social and reproductive crisis? Neither the demographic prevalence of the conjugal, nuclear family, nor the degree to which it is acclaimed or execrated as an ideal, alters the *fact* that family structures may differ in the opportunities they extend to growing children. There are few other bodies of data in which the weight is so decisively one side of the issue.

Recent estimates strongly indicate that the numbers of children with psychosocial disorders has grown over the same time as families have increasingly fractured and fragmented.[21] A correlation is not, of course a causal relationship, except that study after study suggests that children who grow up with both original parents are, on the whole, better off than children living with single or step-parents,[22] whether in terms of health, school performance, intellectual development, behavioural and emotional problems, law-breaking, leaving home early, employment, drug taking, early pregnancy and other measures.

Nowhere are the differences more marked than in the area of mortality and morbidity. Lone parenthood is the strongest socio-demographic predictor of childhood injury, and the hospital admission rate for children of lone parents is twice that of children in two-parent families, while the risk of pedestrian injury is over 50 per cent higher. Indeed, the death rate for children aged 0-15 years of lone parents on Income Support is 42 per cent higher than for children in social class V, the poorest socio-economic group, which includes unemployed and other two-parent families living below the poverty line.[23]

Children from backgrounds of family disruption form a majority of the victims of all kinds of abuse and neglect and three out of four children entering the care system have lone parents.[24] Indeed, the 'most striking feature of all' about the backgrounds of children going into care, is the way these 'magnify... accelerating social trends in a most vivid and exaggerated way' in the degree to which their families are 'incomplete, disrupted, or restructured following earlier breakdowns'.[25] Children are particularly likely to go into care following a crisis when the family is 'reconstituting' itself.

If parental absence and family breakdown put more children on a downward course than would otherwise be the case so, by much the same token, fewer children are removed from disadvantage. The 'quite remarkable' difference in family situations between children who do well by their 20s, particularly educationally, despite the worst backgrounds in terms of income and housing, is the fact that they stay with two original parents.[26]

Patterns of disadvantage are intergenerational. As seen in our National Survey of Sexual Attitudes and Lifestyles, as everywhere else, young women are more likely to become teenage mothers if they have lived with only one parent as a child.[27] Men and women whose parents have divorced cohabit more readily and dissolve their marriages more quickly. This effect on future family formation suggests a dynamic that will progressively weaken the prevalence of unbroken families and, in exposing more children to circumstances likely to have negative consequences for their development, undermine the life chances of future generations. An important aspect of this cycle is the way in which family dislocation may make a disproportionate contribution to persistent and cumulative poverty and welfare dependency. Compared with poor two-parent families, lone parents may not be very successful in improving their circumstances: marital status has become a powerful predictor of time on public assistance.

Cohabitations which produce children feed into this cycle of family disruption at four-fold the rate for marriage.[28] Even teenage mothers who had a child within marriage are more likely to still be with their first 'partner' in their 30s than those who began parenthood as cohabitees: one-in-two compared to one-in-three. Cohabiting mothers also had the most 'partners'—18 per cent had three or more compared to five per cent of teenage married mothers—and, like those who had a child on their own, are far more likely to be living on Income Support.[29]

Since cohabitations also terminate more quickly than marriages, nearly 80 per cent of children of cohabiting parents were under five when their parents parted in a recent study: almost double the rate of formerly married parents.[30] Formerly married fathers provide support at more than double the rate (64 per cent) of former cohabitees or men who have never lived with the mother, and much the same is true of continued, committed contact with the children. Only 10 per cent of formerly married fathers in full-time work and living on their own paid nothing, compared to nearly a third of former cohabitees and never-together men in the same circumstances.

Looking-glass Logic

Does this not indicate that marriage represents a greater commitment and 'a higher degree of investment in the parental relationship', than in the case of cohabitees and never-together couples? But, by reasoning which can only now be described as perverse, the researchers involved emphasize that they 'are not arguing that marriage *causes* higher stability and commitment'. God forbid! Apparently, marriage just symbolises an 'achieved degree of economic security', or is just a 'reflection' of economic conditions. So it is an illusion that it supports parenthood, since people marry when their 'socio-economic circumstances are such that their chances of providing the most favourable social capital for their children are at their highest'. In turn, it is only the 'socio-economic status of the parents rather than the formal relationships' which affects the social capital they provide for their children.[31] Having made marriage disappear as a variable, concern over 'saving' marriages is 'misplaced'—there being nothing to save.

It may be the case that cohabiting parents have a less successful socio-economic profile than married parents; that the less successful cohabitees are more prone to instability than those cohabitees who enjoy better socio-economic conditions, just as the less materially successful among the married are particularly vulnerable to divorce. If economic circumstances worsen from one year to the other, both have a 50 per cent greater chance of breaking up, and conversely, a 50 per cent greater chance of surviving if conditions improve. However, the greater propensity of married parents to stay together cannot be just 'a function of their relatively more successful circumstances'[32] when—after all economic and other factors are controlled—cohabiting parents still break up at double the rate of married couples.[33]

While economic considerations are important to the establishment and durability of marriages, this does not make the two synonymous. Marriage is an institution which, like others, embodies and sustains systems of meaning; organises and stabilises various practices and arrangements; and provides people with reference points outside their own consciousness that give coherence and continuity to their efforts. Cohabitation rests on 'the refusal to make a commitment to the mutual care and shared resources of a family, which in turn generates the expectation that "family-like" relationships are temporary, and so unworthy of the investment of time and energy'.[34] Uncertain prospects may encourage the avoidance of marriage in favour of casual and conditional relationships, precisely because these enable those involved to keep their options open.

The claim that the success rates of different 'family forms' can be accounted for by the resources with which they are identified is little more than a re-statement of the claim that the comparative disadvantages of children of divorced families or single parents are owed entirely to differences in their economic status.

But it is not the case that outcomes are the same for children at an equivalent financial level. The US National Health Interview Survey on Child Health is typical. Involving 17,110 children aged 17 or under, it found that anti-social behaviour, anxiety and depression, headstrong behaviour, hyperactivity, dependency, peer conflict or social withdrawal were higher at lower income levels, and then tended to diminish up the income scale for children in all circumstances. However, within income bands, the differences between children from different family types persisted.[35] Parallel data from the UK's National Child Development Study explored the relationships between children's parenting experiences and what happened to them in adult life. There was a gradient of risk, where children brought up by both birth parents had the lowest risk for psychological problems at every age, followed by restructured families, and lone parents.[36] Even should adverse economic circumstances lead to the formation of lone-parent households, conditions are created in which children are *more vulnerable all the time*.[37] Thus, at a macro level, low per capita income and poverty relate to delinquency, crime and violence indirectly through family breakdown, unmarried births and female-headed households.

There is a temptation to suppress what you don't like. It is alarming to hear calls for a shutdown on investigations or reports on outcomes for children from different family backgrounds, in order to advance the 'de-stigmatising' of lone parents. Of course, the attempts to play down any adverse consequences for children from family disintegration have been as tediously familiar over the years as the denials of family decline. We hear that nothing is amiss because not all children from disrupted families are affected: 'problems are 50 per cent more prevalent among the children of divorce. Yet the fact remains that *most* children of divorced parents do *not* display such problems'.[38] We are told that we cannot infer that children would have done better if their parents had stayed together and even that 'the most careful studies suggest that it is not the loss of a parent, but a hostile emotional environment preceding this loss that causes most of the emotional damage to children'.[39] Contrary to findings that family reorganisation, particularly when it involves one parent's departure, is a strong adverse factor in the lives of children involved in marital breakup, there is reluctance to admit that divorce might have its own dynamics.[40] Instead it 'should be seen as a long-term process commencing prior to separation, that may include; marital conflict, family dysfunction, poor parenting, which regardless of whether or not parents separate are significant factors in children's behaviour problems'.[41] Thus, family structure is not a factor in children's well-being, compared with 'processes' and circumstances. Citing the Home Office's Youth Lifestyles survey, *Social Focus on Families* reports how adolescents who lived with a lone or step-parent were more likely to say that they had offended than those who had lived with both natural parents. However, it sternly reminds us that:

> It is important to note that this does not necessarily mean that coming from a particular type of family structure causes criminal behaviour, because there are numerous other factors to be taken into account. In particular, once the quality of relationships with parents and their willingness to supervise their children were taken into account, the influence of family structures disappears. Among boys

and girls who said that they had a bad relationship with their fathers, the rates admitting to having ever offended were double those of young people who claimed to have had a good relationship. Similarly, in relation to supervision, 32 per cent of boys and girls who were closely supervised admitted offending compared with 53 per cent and 30 per cent respectively for those who were not.[42]

It should not be necessary to make the obvious point that intact marriages have important indirect effects by strongly affecting the probability, even the possibility, that a child will have a good relationship with a father, and that two concerned adults are, on average, more likely to provide adequate supervision than one. (Not surprisingly, communications are worst between adolescents and non-resident fathers, being frustrating and painful for teenagers.[43]) As one American commentator puts it: 'it borders on educational malpractice to tell students that process matters, but structure does not, as if these concepts were somehow competitors for our ideological allegiance, rather than descriptions of two closely interrelated aspects of family life'.[44]

Even after controlling for a variety of factors, an intact marriage in itself makes a positive difference to a child's well-being. After all the attempts to relate economic conditions and child and family characteristics prior to divorce to the long-term outcomes for adults from the National Child Development Study, the effects still would not go away. Pre-existing financial hardship and behavioural problems contributed to the way that those who had experienced parental divorce before 16 years were almost twice as likely to lack formal qualifications as others, but made no difference to men's comparative lack of higher level qualifications. Parental divorce also amplified the risk of unemployment for men and, if one in 16 children of divorce went on to experience homelessness as an adult, compared with one in 28 whose parents stayed together, the risk for women was somewhat reduced by economic considerations, but hardly at all for men. Controlling for childhood hardship, social group and earlier behaviour made little or no difference to the high propensity of both women and men from disrupted families to begin their first live-in relationship in their teens; or for women to be almost twice as likely to be teenage mothers and to give birth while single or cohabiting. Background variables made virtually no difference to the way in which those who had experienced parental divorce were also a lot more likely to have their own first marriage or cohabitation break up. Remarkably, 33 per cent of men who had experienced parental divorce had dissolved their own marriage by their early 30s compared with 18 per cent whose parents had stayed together. But the researcher remains to be convinced that there is anything to bother much about: 'avoiding divorce, no doubt, confers benefits on children, but the magnitude of these benefits are not so large if the conditions that may lead people to divorce in the first place are taken into account'.[45]

All such disclaimers sit incongruously with 'the challenge' to policy makers 'to ensure that children do not become disadvantaged by the structure of the family in which they are brought up'.[46] The usual panacea is an immense umbrella of social work and other supports. To become 'fully-functional', the 'alternative family lifestyles' require a complex of remedial measures, or substitutes for what the two-parent family is more likely to supply as a matter of course.

Maintaining Order?

And very expensive it will be. In theory, at least, two parents can cover the tasks of child rearing between them. For lone parents, the state must take over either the maintenance or the care of the children—or both. In turn, compensatory resources for lone parents represent a major shift of personal services into the public domain. In spite of that, it is difficult to see how any amount of public investment in children could possibly offset the private disinvestment that accompanies the decline of marriage. For example, how is it meant to compensate for ways in which marital and family disruption reduce the linkages in the network of social control and social support, which enable communities to function? Social control is dependent upon more than the individual child's family, and a 'mass' effect is apparent in the way in which the percentage of lone-parent households in a community is predictive of serious crime, or how growing up in neighbourhoods with high rates of family fragmentation trebles, rather than doubles, the likelihood that boys with lone mothers will engage in criminal activity.[47]

Instead of neighbourhood standards being enforced by fathers, low marriage rates mean a decline of the responsible male and an increasing likelihood that men are going to be net contributors to the community's problems. A man who does not recognise the claims of dependents often loses those external demands on himself which could raise him above immediate or short-term desires.[48] This is the reality which underpins the way in which the percentages of the population divorced, households headed by women, and unattached individuals in the community are among the most powerful predictors of crime rates.[49] Men's disengagement from families is of immense and fundamental significance for public order and economic productivity. This is something which is only just beginning to be acknowledged—as we blithely head for a situation in which 54 per cent of men aged 30-34 will be on their own by 2016.[50]

The Depletion of Social Capital

The obverse of family disruption and contraction also tends to be low rates of participation in community activities and organisa-tions on the part of lone mothers and single men compared to married women and fathers.[51] The role of family man is not just a protective against bad behaviour, it is also the basis of a positive contribution to the community. Its absence may weaken general processes of care and education in society, through which one generation exerts itself on behalf of another. Committed kinship is the foremost reservoir of altruistic social involvement, and shapes the moral capital of the next generation.[52] As emphasized by Francis Fukuyama in The End of Order,[53] liberal, democratic, market societies are not self-sustaining but depend upon relations of trust and social virtues like responsibility and duty that they do not generate. But the process whereby moral values, self-sacrifice and social order have been passed down through generations is being disrupted, as the institutions through which society replaces itself—the foremost of which is marriage—are allowed to crumble.

Who's Going To Care?

The far-reaching environmental implications of increasing numbers of people living alone—in terms of land for 4.4 million new homes—might well be described as a 'nightmare scenario' by the Campaign for the Protection of Rural England. What is not quite so keenly appreciated is that it is far more cost-effective for everything from water supplies to home helps if people live together. Atomization means mounting pressure on resources to meet the welfare needs of adults as much as children. When a couple marry, they initiate a whole series of exchanges involving two groups of people. As marriage creates affiliative and integrative patterns, it also constitutes a personal social security system, or network of obligated kin. Parents who experience marital breakdown are less likely to feel supported by relatives compared with intact families, and their own obligations to in-laws are substantially weakened after divorce.[54] Children of divorced families report weaker relationships with both parents in adulthood; are less likely to perceive parents as sources of emergency assistance; and report receiving less help.[55]

If anything, it will be even more costly for public services to replace the missing kin at the end of life than at the beginning, as the aged themselves also disproportionately become the product of falling marriage rates, rising divorce and increasing childlessness. As the foremost source of actual care in old age is a spouse, it is not surprising that the risks of institutionalisation are higher for the never-married. Moreover, regardless of family background, the key person to whom people expect, and prefer, to turn for assistance is overwhelmingly a spouse—just as they expect the family generally to help.[56] Researchers obedient to the party line on the unassailability of the 'new family diversity' are at an even greater loss when it comes to what might be done when people are 'at risk of losing the support of their wider family' in later, compared to earlier, life. The 'challenge' is, it seems, to 'help individuals... create and retain childhood networks', or draw support 'perhaps from family-type neighbourhood relationships'.[57] It certainly will be quite a challenge, as nobody knows what these are meant to be.

None of this might matter if atomised people needed less support, or had less problems—but they do not. The divorced and single of both sexes are far more likely to enter psychiatric hospitals or use outpatient psychiatric services compared to their married counterparts.[58] The same *anomie* is manifest in the strong relationships between the suicides of adults and children, out-of-wedlock births, the divorce rate and the number of persons living alone.[59] While there are positive benefits in marriage for both sexes, much of the health increment for men stems from the dramatic drop in risky behaviour—such as drug and alcohol use—that follows from marriage, but not necessarily cohabitation.[60]

Men uninvolved with families also tend to have poorer work records, having less incentive to work hard, or at all, especially in lower grade or unsatisfying jobs, and are far more likely to become dependent themselves. The relationships between men's marital status, employment and wages are two-way and two-fold. Male marriageability depends much upon having an income which might go some way towards supporting a home, but marriage and fatherhood have a dramatic and positive impact upon male economic activity as well as on social responsibility, motivating men to be more successful in the labour market, and stimulating human capital investment.[61] This has a general effect on wealth creation and productivity, where marriage is related to a whole complex of behaviour basic to economic development. It is something to which those who are beginning to worry about the drop in the male labour supply and the repercussions for future growth might well attend.

While the effects of family breakdown are already apparent, acceptance of the end of marriage and decline of the family is premature. The first step towards recovery is to stop describing social changes as though they were inevitable.

Notes

Miriam E. David

1   *Excellence in Schools*, London: HMSO: Cm 3681:3.

Kathleen Kiernan

1   Kiernan, K. and Estaugh, V., *Cohabitation, Extra-marital Childbearing and Social Policy*, Occasional Paper No. 17, London: Family Policy Studies Centre, 1993.

2   Agell, A., 'Cohabitation without marriage in Swedish law', in Eekelaar, J.M. and Katz, S.N. (eds.), *Marriage and Cohabitation in Contemporary Societies: Areas of Legal, Social and Ethical Change*, Toronto: Butterworths, 1980.

3   Kiernan, K., 'Partnership behaviour in Europe: recent trends and issues', in Coleman, D. (ed.), *Europe's Population*, Oxford University Press, 1996.

4   Ford, R., Marsh, A. and Finlayson, L., *What Happens to Lone Parents: A Cohort Study 1991-95*, London: Policy Studies Institute, 1996.

5   White, L.K. and Booth, A., 'The quality and stability of remarriages: the role of step-children', *American Sociological Review*, Vol. 50, No. 5, 1985.

6   Buchanan, C., Maccoby, E.E. and Dornbusch, S.M., *Adolescents after Divorce*, London: Harvard University Press, 1996.

7   Hetherington, E.M. and Clingempeel, W.G., *Coping with Marital Transitions*, Monographs of the Society for Research in Child Development, Vol. 57, 1992, pp. 2-3.

8   Kiernan, K., 'The Legacy of Parental Divorce: social, economic and demographic experiences in adulthood', ESRC: Centre for Analysis of Social Exclusion, London School of Economics CASE Paper No.1, 1997.

9   Ford, *et al., op. cit.*

10 *The NICHD Early Child Care Research Network*, Washington DC: National Institute of Child Health and Development 1997.

11 Kempeneers, M. and Lelievre, E., *Employment and the Family: Eurobarometer, 34: 1990*, Brussels: European Commission, 1992.

Patricia Morgan

1   Clarke, L. and Burghes, L., 'Cohabitation: a threat to family stability?', *Family Policy Bulletin*, London: Family Policy Studies Centre, July 1995.

2   Research Results No 2, ESRC, June 1997.

84   THE FRAGMENTING FAMILY: DOES IT MATTER?

3   Popenoe, D., 'The national family wars', *Journal of Marriage and the Family*, Vol. 55, August 1993, pp. 553-55.

4   See 'Beware of a moral agenda', *Independent on Sunday*, 7 December 1997.

5   Buchanan, A. and Ten Brinke, J., *What Happened When They Were Grown Up?*, York: Joseph Rowntree Foundation, 1997, p. x.

6   See, for example, Bumpass, L., 'The declining significance of marriage: changing family life in the United States', Keynote Address, *Changing Britain*, Economic and Social Research Council, Issue One, November 1994; and Maclean, M. and Eekelaar, J., *The Parental Obligation*, Oxford: Hart Publishing, 1997.

7   Hobcraft, J. and Kiernan, K., *Becoming a Parent in Europe*, Welfare State Programme/116, London: Suntory-Toyota International Centre for Economics and Related Disciplines, 1995.

8   Newman, P. and Smith, A., *Social Focus on Families*, Office for National Statistics, London: HMSO, 1997, p. 54.

9   *Ibid.*, p. 46.

10 Hobcraft and Kiernan, *Becoming a Parent in Europe, op. cit.*, p. 3.

11 Bumpass, 'The declining significance of marriage: changing family life in the United States', Keynote Address, *Changing Britain, op. cit.*, p. 9.

12 Popenoe, D., 'American family decline, 1960-1990: a review and appraisal', *Journal of Marriage and the Family*, Vol. 55, August 1993, pp. 527-555.

13 Blackstone, Sir W., *Commentaries on the Laws of England*, Book 1, quoted in Maclean and Eekelaar, *The Parental Obligation, op. cit.*, p. 33.

14 Malinowski, B. (ed.), *Sex and Repression in Savage Society*, 1927, reprinted Routledge and Kegan Paul, 1960, pp. 212-13.

15 Maclean and Eekelaar, *op. cit.*, p. 8.

16 *Ibid.*

17 McGlone, F., Park, A. and Roberts, C., 'Relative values: kinship and friendship', in Jowell, R., Curtice, J., Park, A., Brook, L. and Thomson, K. (eds.), *British Social Attitudes, The 13th Report*, Aldershot: Dartmouth, 1996.

18 Hoggett, B., 'Ends and means: the utility of marriage as a legal institution', in Eekelaar, J. and Katz, S.N. (eds.), *Marriage and Cohabitation in Contemporary Societies: Areas of Legal, Social and Ethical Change*, Toronto: Butterworths, 1980, quoted in Maclean and Eekelaar, *op. cit.*, p. 10.

19 Ford, R. and Millar, J., 'Private lives and public responses: lone parenthood and future policy', *Foundations*, York: Joseph Rowntree Foundation, July 1997, p. 2.

20 Dewar, J., *Law and the Family*, London: Butterworths, 1992, quoted in Maclean and Eekelaar, *op. cit.*, p. 10.

21 Rutter, M. and Smith, D. (eds.), *Psychosocial Disorders in Young People: Time Trends and their Causation*, Chichester: John Wiley & Sons, 1995.

22 Booth, A. and Dunn, J., *Stepfamilies: Who Benefits? Who Does Not?* Hilldale, NJ: Lawrence Erlbaum, 1994.

23 Judge, K. and Benzeval, M., 'Health inequalities: new concerns about the children of single mothers', *British Medical Journal*, Vol. 306, 13 March 1993; Roberts, I. and Pless, B., 'Social policy as a cause of childhood accidents: the children of lone mothers', *British Medical Journal*, Vol. 311, 7 October 1995.

24 Packman, J. with Randall, J. and Jacques, N., *Who Needs Care?*, Oxford: Basil Blackwell, 1986, p. 32; see also Bebbington, A. and Miles, J., 'The background of children who enter local authority care', *British Journal of Social Work*, Vol. 19, 1989, pp. 349-68.

25 Packman, *Who Needs Care?*, *op. cit.*, p. 34.

26 Pilling, D., *Escape from Disadvantage*, London: Falmer Press, 1990.

27 Population and Household Change Research results, Economic and Social Research Council, No. 4, June 1997

28 Buck, N. and Ermisch, J., 'Cohabitation in Britain', *Changing Britain*, Issue 3, Economic and Social Research Council, October 1995; McKay, S., 'New data on life events: the family and working lives survey', *Changing Britain*, Issue 7, Economic and Social Research Council, October 1997.

29 Kiernan, K.E., *Transition to Parenthood: Young Mothers, Young Fathers: Associated Factors and Later Life Experiences*, Discussion paper Welfare State Programme/113, London: Suntory and Toyota International Centres for Economics and Related Disciplines, London School of Economics, 1995.

30 Maclean and Eekelaar, *The Parental Obligation, op. cit.*,

31 *Ibid.*, p. 143.

32 *Ibid.*, p. 143.

33 Ermisch, J., University of Essex, November 1997, personal communication.

34 Carlson, A., 'Liberty, order and the family', Davies, J. (ed.), *The Family: Is It Just Another Lifestyle Choice?*, London: IEA Health and Welfare Unit, 1993, p. 53.

35 Dawson, D.A., *Family Structure and Children's Health: United States 1988*, Series 10: 178, Vital and Health Statistics, Maryland: US Department of Health and Human Services, 1991; Pilling, D., *Escape from Disadvantage*, London: The Falmer Press, 1990.

36 Buchanan and Ten Brinke, *What Happened When They Were Grown Up?, op. cit.*

37 Lempers, J.D., Lempers, D.C. and Simons, R.L., 'Economic hardship, parenting and distress in adolescence', *Child Development*, Vol. 60, 1989, pp. 25-39; Takeuchi, D.T., Williams, D.R. and Adair, R.K., 'Economic stress in the family and children's emotional and behavioural problems', *Journal of Marriage and the Family*, Vol. 53, 1991, pp. 1,031-41; Jones, L., 'Unemployment and child abuse', *Families in Society: The Journal of Contemporary Human Services*, 1990, pp. 579-87.

38 Utting, D., 'Happy families', *Search*, 16 June 1993, Joseph Rowntree, p. 14.

39 Stacey J., 'Good riddance to "The Family": a response to David Popenoe', *Journal of Marriage and the Family*, Vol. 55, 1993, p. 546.

40 Tripp, J. and Cockett, M., *The Exeter Family Study: Family Breakdown and its Effects on Children*, University of Exeter, 1994.

41 Kiernan, K., *The Legacy of Parental Divorce: Social, Economic and Demographic Experiences in Adulthood*, Centre for Analysis of Social Exclusion, CASE paper 1, London School of Economics, 1997, p. 2.

42 Newman and Smith, *Social Focus on Families, op. cit.*, p. 57.

43 Coleman, J., *Key Data on Adolescence*, Trust for the Study of Adolescence, 1997.

44 Glenn, N., *Closed Hearts, Closed Minds: The Textbook Story of Marriage*, New York: Institute for American Values, 1997, p. 22.

45 Kiernan, K., *The Legacy of Parental Divorce: Social, Economic and Demographic Experiences in Adulthood, op. cit.*, p. 39.

46 Buchanan and Ten Brinke, *What Happened When They Were Grown Up?, op. cit.*, p. 29.

47 Sampson, R. J., 'Crime in cities: the effects of formal and informal social control', in Reiss, Jnr., A.J. and Tony, M. (eds.), *Communities and Crime*, Vol. 8, in *Crime and Justice*, University of Chicago Press, 1987. Sampson, R.J., 'Does an intact family reduce burglary risks for neighbours?', *Sociology and Social Research*, Vol. 71, 1987, pp. 404-07.

48 Dench, G., *From Extended Family to State Dependency*, Centre for Community Studies, Middlesex University, 1993, p. 7.

49 Gottfredson, M.R. and Hirschi, T., *A General Theory of Crime*, California: Stanford University Press, 1990.

50 Newman and Smith, *Social Focus on Families, op. cit.*

51 Sampson, R.J., 'Urban black violence: the effect of male joblessness and family disruption', *American Journal of Sociology*, Vol. 93, No. 2, 1987, pp. 348-82.

52 Snarey, J. *et al.*, 'The role of parenting in men's psychosocial development: a longitudinal study of early adulthood infertility and midlife generativity', *Developmental Psychology*, Vol. 23, No. 4, 1987, pp. 593-603; and Sundeen, R.A., 'Family life course status and volunteer behaviour', *Sociological Perspectives*, Vol. 33, No. 4, 1990, pp. 483-500.

53 Fukuyama, F., *The End of Order*, London: Social Market Foundation, 1997.

54 Coleman, M., Ganong, L. and Cable, S., 'Beliefs about women's intergenerational family obligations to provide support before and after divorce and remarriage', *Journal of Marriage and the Family*, Vol. 59, No. 1, 1997.

55 White, L., 'Growing up with single parents and stepparents: long term effects on family solidarity', *Journal of Marriage and the Family* Vol. 56, No. 3, November 1994, pp. 935-48.

56 McGlone, F., Park, A. and Roberts, C., 'Relative values: kinship and friendship', *British Social Attitudes, The 13th Report*, edited by Jowell, R., Curtice, J., Park, A., Brook, L. and Thomson, K., Aldershot: Dartmouth, 1996; McGlone, F., *Disability and Dependency in Old Age: A Demographic and Social Audit*, London: Family Policy Studies Centre, 1992.

57 Buchanan and Ten Brinke, *What Happened When They Were Grown Up?, op. cit.*, pp. 43, 79.

58 Dominian, J. *et al.*, *Marital Breakdown and the Health of the Nation*, London: One Plus One, 1991, pp. 13, 16-17.

59 Breault, K.D., 'Suicide in America: the test of Durkheim's theory of religious and family integration, 1933-1980', *American Journal of Sociology*, Vol. 92, 1986, pp. 651-52.

60 Lillard, L.A. and Waite, L.J., 'Til death do us part: marital disruption and mortality', *American Journal of Sociology*, Vol.100, 1995, pp. 1131-56.

61 Teachman, J.D., Call, V.R.A. and Price Carver, K., 'Marital status and the duration of joblessness among white men', *Journal of Marriage and the Family*, Vol. 56, 1994, pp. 415-28.